B. F. Skinner From A to Z

W. Joseph Wyatt

Third Millennium Press
Hurricane, WV

B.F. Skinner from A to Z

For information address: Third Millennium Press
P. O. Box 844, Hurricane, WV 25526

Printing History
First Printing 2001

TMP Books are published by Third Millennium Press
P. O. Box 844, Hurricane, WV 25526

The name "TMP" and the   TMP   logo are

trademarks belonging to Third Millennium Press

Printed in the United States of America
10 9 8 7 6 5 4 3 2 1

Library of Congress Control No. 00-133706
ISBN (Softbound): 0-9663622-2-5
ISBN (Hardbound): 0-9663622-5-X

Ordering Information - See Final Page

B. F. Skinner From A to Z

To My Mentor & Friend
Rob Hawkins

Also by W. Joseph Wyatt
The Millennium Man

See final page for ordering information

B. F. Skinner From A to Z

Table of Contents

A note on organization of this book: The superscripts that follow each quotation refer to the numbered references found beginning on page 146

W. Joseph Wyatt

Preface

Well over one hundred direct quotations by B.F. Skinner are presented. They are taken from his books and papers written from the 1940s to the 1990s. Each is followed by an explanatory Author's Note. Quotations are arranged alphabetically and provide a dictionary of representative statements by Skinner about topics from A (Aggression) to Z (Zen and Zoosemiotics). In between are Skinner's thoughts about classroom discipline, common sense, ethics, genetics, love, meaning, psychotherapy, religion, science, war, and many more. The quotations are intended to put the reader in direct touch with both Skinner's writing and with behavior analysis to the extent that Skinner's writing reflects it. It is hoped that misconceptions about Skinner and about behavior analysis will be dispelled as well. A brief review of the highlights of Skinner's life and career is included.

Why This Book?

Shortly after his death on August 18, 1990 at age 86 B. F. Skinner was called, "The greatest contemporary psychologist...living history," by American Psychological Association CEO Raymond D. Fowler.

A week before he died Dr. Skinner made his last public appearance, in Boston, to receive an award from APA, its Citation for Outstanding Lifetime Contribution to Psychology. He was the first person to receive that award in the 100 year history of the organization. In presenting the award APA President Stanley R. Graham praised Skinner as a creative scientist, a pioneer in psychology, an intellectual leader, as a person sensitive to the human condition, and as a citizen of the world who provided us with, "thoughtful, often provocative, and always compassionate insights into such uniquely human endeavors as ethics, freedom, dignity, governance, and peace."

Presented here are brief quotations on a number of topics by B.F. Skinner. I have selected them to enable the reader to briefly be touched by some of Skinner's ideas. An author's note follows each quotation. The notes place the quotations in context and explain the points Skinner was addressing. Now subsumed under the general term behavior analysis, Skinner's philosophy and his laboratory science contain a number of fundamental terms, concepts and principles. His thoughts on these may be found in the following: behavior as subject matter; behaviorism; consequences; contingency of reinforcement; control of human behavior; experimental analysis of behavior; functional analysis; lawfulness of behavior; lower animals, study of; operant; punishment; quantity of behavior;

W. Joseph Wyatt

reinforcement; single subject experimentation; and youth of behavior analysis.

Some issues are of general interest in the behavioral and related sciences. A number of these are important for the philosophy of science. Skinner's comments on matters such as free will, responsibility and value judgement have stirred substantial debate. See the following: autonomous man; consciousness; dignity; epistemology; ethics and morals; freedom; free will; higher mental processes; insight; intuition; knowing; knowledge; self-knowledge; man, the machine; meaning; mind; purpose; responsibility; self-control; survival of cultures; value judgements; voluntary and involuntary behavior.

The interplay between theoretical positions is a constant in behavioral science. Skinner has given a great deal of thought to the analysis of a far-ranging spectrum of positions other than his own, as well as to those related to behavior analysis: clinical psychology; cognitive science; existentialism; explanatory fiction; higher mental processes; humanistic psychology; Jung, Carl; language development; mentalism; needs; physiologist; self; statistics; theory; thinking; vernacular; yoga; and youth of behavior analysis.

There is little in the richly tinted kaleidoscope of human experience that has escaped Skinner's commentary. See, for example, the following of his analyses. They run the gamut from A (aggression) to Z (Zen and zoosemiotics): aggression; the arts; attention; awareness; benevolence; blame; common sense; conformity; creativity; heroes; knowing; marriage; memories; needs; nervousness; novelists; originality; permissiveness; religion; responsi-bility; the self; smoking; superstition; the unconscious;

understanding; value judgements; verbal behavior; war; welfare; wealth; will; witchcraft; writers; yoga; Zen; and zoosemiotics.

Analysis of the operation of controlling agencies was of great concern to Skinner. Five of these have been of particular interest. They are: government, religion, education, economics and psychotherapy. See: behavior modification; classroom discipline; classroom failure; clinical psychology; college teaching; democracy; economics; education; government; Heaven and Hell; Judeo-Christian tradition; law; psychotherapy; religion; self-control; and teaching machines.

Skinner's view of science, behavioral science, the activities of those who engage in them, and the importance of theory to science are of interest. See: science; scientific behavior; statistics; and theory.

Humor can be found in Skinner's writing, if one knows where to look. See, for example: Pavlov; quotation; Unformalized principle of scientific practice no. 1; Unformalized principle of scientific practice no. 2;

Finally, the quotations herein should dispel several misconceptions about Skinner (and behavior analysis) that are found among lay people and professionals alike:

1.   That Skinner ignores genetic influences on behavior (See aggression, genetics).

2.   That Skinner advocates totalitarianism (see democracy, government).

3.   That Skinner denies the existence of thoughts,

W. Joseph Wyatt

emotions and feelings (see emotion, feeling, higher mental processes, knowing, private events, thinking).

4. That Skinner advocates the use of punishment (see punishment).

5. That Skinner disavows all theory (see theory).

6. That Skinner's theory leaves meaningless such concepts as ethics, morals, or values (see ethics and morals, value judgement).

7. That Skinner ignores the uniqueness of the individual (See Individuality, Uniqueness of the person).

8. That Skinner fails to acknowledge the existence of conscious experience (See awareness).

9. That Skinner would entirely replace teachers with teaching machines (See education).

10. That Skinner is averse to clinical psychology (See clinical psychology).

11. That Skinner's theory robs behavior of its meaning and purpose (see meaning, purpose).

Skinner's Life and Influence

Burrhus Frederic Skinner was born on March 20, 1904 in Susquehanna, Pennsylvania. His father was an attorney for the Erie Railroad. He recalled his mother as bright with strict standards. He described his home during those early years as "warm and stable."

He was influenced to be a writer by his high school English teacher, Miss Graves. After high school Skinner went to Hamilton College where he graduated in 1926.

He then spent an unsuccessful year attempting to be a writer. Then, influenced by his reading of Bertrand Russell, John B. Watson, and Ivan Pavlov, he decided to become a graduate student in psychology. Entering Harvard University in the fall of 1928, Skinner developed close professional and personal ties to fellow graduate student Fred Keller. Their association lasted until Skinner's death.

After receiving his Ph.D. in 1931 Skinner remained at Harvard for five more years, supported by fellowships. In 1936 he left Harvard to become professor at the University of Minnesota. That same year he married Yvonne Blue. They later had two children, Julie, now a professor at West Virginia University and a recognized behavior analyst, and Deborah, an artist living in London.

The Behavior of Organisms, Skinner's first book, was published in 1938. Seven years later he left Minnesota to become chairman of the Psychology Department at Indiana University. His second book, the utopian novel *Walden II*, was written the summer just prior to his arrival at Indiana in the fall of 1945, but was not published until 3 years later. That same year Skinner returned to Harvard where he remained until his retirement.

W. Joseph Wyatt

While at Harvard he published *Science and Human Behavior* in 1953 which some scholars feel is the single work that best states his philosophy of behaviorism. Many other books followed. They included *Verbal Behavior* in 1957, and two which set his theory in terms suitable for the thoughtful layperson: *Beyond Freedom and Dignity* in 1971, and *About Behaviorism* in 1974.

Skinner devoted substantial time to the application of the principles of behavior to classroom learning. He developed early versions of teaching machines and programmed textbooks. He also developed applications of behavior analysis that were successfully applied to the psychotic behavior of state hospital patients.

Throughout his career Skinner received many awards and honors: the Distinguished Scientific Contribution Award of the American Psychological Association in 1958, the National Medal of Science in 1968, the International Award of the Joseph P. Kennedy Foundation for Mental Retardation in 1971, the Humanist of the Year Award from the American Humanist Society in 1972, the Award for Distinguished Contributions to Educational Research and Development from the American Education Research Association in 1978, and in 1990, just one week before his death, he became the first recipient of APA's Citation for Lifetime Contribution to Psychology.

Skinner's influence has been substantial. Gilgen (1981) surveyed the authors of 13 books on the history of psychology, asking them to rate the major events and influences in psychology since World War II. "The contributions of B. F. Skinner" tied for second after "The general growth of psychology."

In Another study (Heyduk & Fenigstein, 1984) 92 eminent psychologists were asked to name the authors who most influenced their own work. Among those responding who received their doctorates after 1951, Skinner was most frequently cited.

Professor Skinner died on August 18, 1990 one day after he penned the final changes in a paper that later was published in *American Psychologist* (Skinner, 1990). That journal, which is the flagship publication of the American Psychological Association, devoted a special issue to Skinner two years later (Lattal, 1992).

Gilgen, A.R. (1981). Important people in post World War II American psychology: A survey. *Journal Supplement Abstract Service*, Document no. 2171.

Hayduk, R.G., & Fenigstein, A. (1984). Influential works and authors in psychology: A survey of eminent psychologists. *American Psychologist*, 39, 556-559.

Lattal, K.A. (Ed.) (1992). Reflections on B.F. Skinner and psychology [Special issue]. *American Psychologist*, 47, (11).

Skinner, B.F. (1990). Can psychology be a science of the mind? *American Psychologist*, 45, 1206-1210.

W. Joseph Wyatt

Contemporary Behavior Analysis

Behavior analysis is a natural science approach to the study of behavior, and the application and analysis of science-based interventions to problems of individual, social, and cultural importance.

There are several principles which underlie behavior analysis. The first of these is that behavior is lawful. This means that behavior is caused by something, and even if we do not know the cause it is at least potentially identifiable. Second, the best way to study behavior is scientifically. While science may have its drawbacks and pitfalls, it is still better than non-science. This means that contemporary behavior analysts have put aside prescientific explanations of behavior such as demonology, astrology, and the like. In fact, behavior analysts view the study of behavior as a branch of biology--a specialized branch more interested in studying the functions of organisms than their structure.

Because they believe that behavior is lawful, and because they have rejected prescientific explanations, present day behavior analysts also reject the idea that behavior happens spontaneously, or that it is done randomly. In essence, behavior is determined. That concept brings behavior analysts a great deal of criticism because it means that they reject the notion of free will.

Free will has been an integral part of western democratic philosophy since the founding of the United States. It is the basis of our criminal justice system and is so strongly instilled in us that we may be reluctant to view it as a prescientific explanation of behavior. We are hesitant to consider it in the same class of explanations as demonology and astrology.

Yet, as a behavioral analysis of human activity has progressed there is less and less human activity that remains to be explained by free will. The rejection of free will, however, does not mean that people have no control over their environment. Nor does it mean that they do not engage in decision making. Rather, the rejection of free will simply means that activities such as decision making do not happen freely.

In viewing the study of behavior as a branch of biology behavior analysts operate within the realm of matter and energy, like the other natural sciences. They reject any explanation of behavior which appeals to events outside the realm of matter and energy. This means that behavior analysts reject supernatural explanations of behavior such as ghosts, and this is true whether the ghosts are said to exist in the usual places (old houses, cemeteries) or in the mysterious world of the mind.

Over the years a variety of new names for these ghosts, hobgoblins, and demons have been devised. For example, Freud called them libido, id, ego, and the like. These are frequently said to be made of some different "stuff" that is outside the realm of matter or energy and therefore cannot be observed or measured in any scientific way. This leads one to wonder how Freud "discovered" that such entities exist and could, therefore, cause behavior. And that is exactly the behavior analytic objection to such "mentalistic explanations of behavior."

Behavior analysts view everything that an organism does as the result of the interaction of its unique genetic and environmental histories. They have been accused of ignoring genetic influences on behavior, and that may have been true for an earlier version of behavioral analysis, but it has not been the case for at least 60 years.

Presently behavior analysts recognize that both genetic and environmental variables influence behavior. But genetic variables are less amendable to change and are actually quite unlikely to change in the lifetime of an individual (or even in the lifetimes of several generations of individuals). Therefore, the focus of behavior analysts is on environments and how environments influence behavior.

Theoretical Aspects of Behavior Analysis

Behavior analysis is undergirded by a comprehensive theory. Oddly, it is mistakenly said by some that behavior analysis is anti-theory or the "no-theory" school of thought.

However, it is only certain kinds of theories (those that attempt to explain behavior by appealing to other-worldly phenomena) to which behavior analysts object. The basic building blocks of its theory are contained in the paragraphs above. That is, behavior is lawful, it is best studied scientifically as a branch of biology, and that everything an organism does is the product of the organism's unique genetic and environmental histories.

Sometimes behavior analysts are said to ignore thoughts and feelings or to even deny their existence. That is not the case. Rather, behavior analysts have a unique view of the role of thoughts and feelings. Thoughts and feelings frequently happen at roughly the same time as overt behavior. Because of that timeliness we may mistakenly believe that our overt behavior has been caused by a thought or feeling. For example, it would be quite typical for a

person to say "I went to the library because I felt like it."
However, that would be wrong. What is more likely is that
there were a number of factors in an individual's environmental history (possibly some in his or her genetic history
though that would be unlikely) which accounted for going to
the library. Those same factors also accounted for a certain
feeling that one had in the past when he or she went to the
library. Thus, to say that "I went to the library because I
felt like it" cuts off further inquiry into the real causes of
going. In fact to fully explain it we would need to explain
the variables that influenced one to go to the library *and* the
variables that influenced one to have a particular feeling
while going to the library.

Another area that is important within behavior
analysis is its emphasis on positive means of influencing or
controlling behavior. Whether in education settings, the
workplace, government, or anywhere else most of us would
agree that we would rather be controlled positively than
negatively. That is, we would rather work for a paycheck
or other reward, rather than work to avoid a punishment.
In fact, one of the most widely discussed areas of behavior
analysis, if not all of psychology, is called positive
reinforcement. Behavior analysts believe that people often
do what they do because of the consequences of their
activity in similar situations on previous occasions. Positive
consequences are the preferred vehicle to make us more
likely to engage in healthy, productive activity and are the
consequences that behavior analysts advocate. While there
may be occasions when punitive consequences are
unavoidable and may be successfully used under controlled
conditions, behavior analysts prefer that positive reinforcement be used rather than punishment.

W. Joseph Wyatt

Much experimental research in behavior analysis began with lower animals. Some of the general principles in the field were discovered in studies of lower animals. For example, positive reinforcement was first analyzed experimentally in Skinner's laboratory and in other laboratories using rats and pigeons in the Skinner box. Out of this came the knowledge that there are some similarities between lower animals and humans. For example, the ability to change behavior via positive reinforcement is similar across species, as is the ability to discriminate the differences between situations and the similarities among them.

However, there are enormous differences between humans and lower species as well. For example, humans have a much more favorable ratio of brain-to-body mass than any other species. The result of this is our higher intelligence and our complex abilities to think abstractly, to create language, and to function far beyond the level of lower species.

However, because behavior analysts have pointed out some similarities between humans and lower species some criticism has arisen. It has come from those who feel that behavior analysts are attempting to rob us of our individuality by treating us simply as members of the herd, having no uniqueness. That criticism is wrong. Actually the behavior analytic view is that all organisms are unique because they all have unique environmental histories and all (except identical twins) have unique genetic histories. In short there is nothing anti-individual or anti-democratic about behavior analysis.

Contemporary behavior analysis deals with many of

the rich and complex activities of human existence. These include language and relationships. However the earlier versions of behavior analysis kept it simple. They dealt with simple responses that were easily observed and easily measured. In more recent years more complex human events have been, and continued to be, studied. These include the intricacies of marriage and parent-child relationships and the spectrum of presenting clinical problems.

Finally, there are a number of terms and concepts which are part of the common language, and in varying degrees part of the professional psychological language, that are the source of confusion to some regarding behavior analysis.

For example, some have mistakenly criticized behavior analysis, claiming that it denies concepts like "knowing," and "conscious awareness." In fact behavior analysts readily acknowledge that we know things and that we are consciously aware. At the same time behavior analysts hold that we do not explain anything by saying that we did it because we "knew" how to do it, or because we were "aware" of how to do it. The real causes lie in our genes and in our environment.

Critics have complained that the deterministic view tends to rob us of concepts such as meaning, purpose, intention, ethics, morals, and value judgement. That is inaccurate. The meaning, purpose, or intention of any behavior is generally to be found in its consequences. And ethics, morals, and value judgements are quite real, and very important. But, as with "knowing" and "conscious awareness," they are not explanations of behavior.

People do not do what they do because they have an

W. Joseph Wyatt

ethical sense or a sense of morals or the like. Rather, what is ethical and moral is usually what is approved of by a culture. Ethical traits exist in our cultures, not in ourselves, according to behavior analysts.

The Experimental Analysis of Behavior

The history of basic research in behavior analysis might be said to have begun with the Russian physiologist Ivan Pavlov. He received the Nobel prize in the early 1900s and later did the classic experiments with conditioning. Pavlov conditioned a dog to salivate at the sound of a bell, the bell having previously been paired with the introduction of meat powder to the dog's dish. This brought up a question. If a dog's behavior could be conditioned, why not a person's?

John B. Watson became known as the first behaviorist just a few years later, between 1910 and 1920. Watson took a much more radical view than contemporary behavior analysts when he held that we should not attempt to study unobservable behaviors such as thoughts and feelings. Nevertheless, Watson wrote several seminal papers and books and for a time behaviorism became the dominant approach to child rearing in America. However, Watson went well beyond his data when, for example, he suggested that too much hugging would be bad for the child- -a view that causes most contemporary behavior analysts to shudder. In time, Watson's star fell and B. F. Skinner became the best known proponent of behavior analysis by about 1940.

Skinner had studied Watson and Pavlov and others and was particularly interested in Pavlov's classical conditioning experiments. But Skinner felt that Pavlov was missing one of the most important influences on behavior-- the consequences which follow it. Thus, Skinner studied a type of conditioning which he called "operant" conditioning. He devised the term because he was interested in the way in which an organism operated in its environment to produce consequences that were positively reinforcing.

Skinner began to study rats and pigeons in special cages where they learned to press a bar and receive a bit of food, positive reinforcement. Also Skinner renamed Pavlov's method "respondent conditioning," in reference to the fact that the dog in Pavlov's experiment simply responded to what was presented to him rather than seeking out, or operating upon, elements of its environment in order to produce reinforcement.

In time Skinner expanded his studies to include what he called **schedules of reinforcement**. He found that if an activity such as a bar press by a pigeon or rat was reinforced in every instance with a bite of food the animal would continue with hundreds of bar presses even after the food stopped coming.

But when Skinner varied the schedule of the reinforcement, when he provided the bite of food after every second, third, fourth, tenth, fiftieth bar press, there was even more powerful responding on the part of the rat or pigeon. When a partial schedule of reinforcement was stopped and no more food was given, the rat or pigeon would press the bar far more times, perhaps thousands of times, before giving up. Thus Skinner had discovered a principle which applied to rats and pigeons (and later it would be found to be true for humans as well). Namely, Skinner had learned that a partial schedule of reinforcement created behavior more resistant to extinction than did a continuous schedule of reinforcement.

Skinner went on to study other elements related to learning. These included concepts such as stimulus control, shaping, fading, negative reinforcement and punishment.

Stimulus control refers to the control that any stimulus exerts upon us. An animal in a Skinner box learned, for example, that only when a light was turned on would a bar press result in a bit of food. In time the light controlled the presence or absence of rapid bar pressing. An analogy for humans is what happens when we approach a green light that turns yellow and then red. The light exerts control on us. The red light controls us by causing us to stop. The yellow light controls us by causing us to slow down (or hit the accelerator and hope that we make it through the intersection). The green causes us to proceed.

Shaping refers to the process whereby many very complex behaviors are developed, particularly behaviors which do not initially appear full-blown in their final state. Language is perhaps the best example. The young child is initially approved of, coaxed, stroked, for making any verbalization at all. But in time at least a few of the infant's verbalizations sound like words or the beginnings of words and those get even more attention and approval from doting parents. Gradually the first words are shaped by the differential attention (reinforcement) of the parents. In time the first words are "old hat" to the parents who then pay much more attention when two-word sentences are put together. And the process goes on until complex language is shaped.

The process of **fading** explains why some behaviors, even complex behaviors, continue in the absence of a stimulus that previously had been routinely present. For example, a child learning to write its letters might need a representation of the alphabet beside him or on the board in front of him. But in time that is not as important and the writing may take place in the absence of any written model of the letter being provided to him. In the same way consequences that maintain behavior may be faded out of existence while the behavior continues. For example, consider the "oohs" and "aahs" of a parent who is showing approval for a child's first efforts at potty training. Naturally those reinforcers are quite important in the beginning but they fade from importance as time goes by. Other reinforcers take their place (such as the comfort of having dry pants).

Just as we desire positive reinforcement, we also want **negative reinforcement**. Negative reinforcement results from the removal of something aversive or negative. For example, a crying baby who is being irritated by a wet, soggy diaper may soon find that the crying was negatively reinforced by the removal of the uncomfortable diaper. Naturally this would make the baby more likely to cry again the next time it has a soggy diaper, and that is highly adaptive and healthy for the baby.

Negative reinforcement also describes at least some of the reasons why drug addiction is a powerful habit not easily broken. Attempts to quit using the drug cause uncomfortable internal stimuli to occur. These include anxiety, depression, stomach cramps, and others. An addict who then gets rid of this discomfort by taking another hit of his drug has just engaged in negative reinforcement. His drug taking was negatively reinforced (and is therefore more likely to occur again) because it removed the aversive feelings of withdrawal.

Skinner and those in other labs over the past 50 years have also investigated the influence of **punishment**.

However, Skinner and most behavior analysts view punishment as something not to be used, or to be used only under carefully controlled conditions and as a last resort. This is because punishment might easily be abused, and it often creates anxiety and can cause the punished individual to fight back against the punisher.

While Skinner was doing laboratory studies of animals he also began to devote his attention to some applications with humans. For example, Skinner looked at the influence of reinforcement on the psychotic talk and actions of patients at Metropolitan State Hospital in Massachusetts. He found that the frequency of psychotic activity was reduced by reinforcing normal talk with candy and cigarettes.

Thus, Skinner had taken principles he had learned in the laboratory and applied them directly to the betterment of people. Another such incident began with Skinner's visit to his daughter's elementary school classroom on parents' day. There he noticed a teacher who, though possessed of the best of intentions, was violating virtually every principle of behavior. Skinner went home and began working to develop a teaching machine. With his machine small frames of material were presented to the student who then was asked questions by the machine. This was a forerunner of computer learning packages. The student had the opportunity to answer a question and get immediate feedback, positive or negative, by the message that appeared on the screen.

Presently contemporary behavior analysts continue a rich variety of experimental research. They are studying such complex activities as language and verbal behavior, stimulus equivalence (that is, the ways in which stimuli that

W. Joseph Wyatt

are similar, but not precisely alike, may get the same response from an organism) and a variety of clinical disorders.

Applied Behavior Analysis

Beyond its theoretical underpinnings and its history of basic research with both lower animals and humans, there is a vast and growing literature dealing with applications of behavior analytic research to important problems of everyday human experience.

This body of research shows that behavior analytic treatment methods can be used to improve the lives of retarded and autistic individuals, can vastly improve classroom conduct and academic performance for the troubled student and the normal student alike, can be highly useful in improving parenting styles and decreasing the likelihood of child abuse and neglect, and have useful applications in many other settings including business and industry, correctional facilities, and, of course, therapy clinics.

Applied behavior analysis has reached the point that its technology has become highly diversified and specialized and it has become nearly impossible for one to keep up with it.

The breath and scope of the influence of contemporary applied behavior analysis is evident in the program offerings of the annual conference of the Association for Behavior Analysis International--the primary international organization dealing with behavior analytic theory, experimentation and applications. ABAI offers special interest groups for those whose primary expertise is in working with autistic individuals, those in corrections, education, gerontology, and other areas. A recent convention program included offerings in areas such as treating panic disorder, managing organizations, women's issues, drug addiction, environmental clean up, AIDS prevention, relationship skills, treatment of habit disorders such as smoking and overeating, as well as treatment of depression and anxiety and a host of other real world problems.

For example, a recent behavior analytic gerontological treatment (Bourgeois, 1990) involved the use of study sessions and stimulus wallets for Alzheimer's disease sufferers. The patients were given wallets that contained pictures of family members and other familiar stimuli, and then were provided with daily training sessions in which they practiced recognizing the faces and other information contained in the wallet. The result was impressive. After several weeks of training, the patients receiving the training were much better at recalling the important details of their lives than were those who had not had the benefit of the training.

Consider another example of recent behavior analytic research. We all have noticed that some children seem easily able to exercise self-control, while others are highly impulsive. Likely we have wondered wherein lies the difference. This was the focus of research by Irene Grote and Donald Baer (1991) at the University of Kansas. They worked with twenty-one children between the ages of two and six. They gave the children opportunities to choose between a small "reinforcer" (one sticker, or one page from a book read to them) immediately or a larger reinforcer (two stickers or several pages read to them) later. Seven of the children consistently chose the immediate enjoyment over waiting for something better. But then the researchers taught the children (by means of an hourglass) more about the actual time they would have to wait in order to get a larger number of stickers or pages read to them.

Once the children had learned that, they began to show greater preference for the delayed activity and were able to tolerate even longer delays as the training continued.

Grote and Baer feel that such experimentation will uncover the reasons that some children seem to possess a great deal of "self-control" while others seem possessed by a great deal of "impulsiveness."

Conclusions

Behavior analysis is a broad philosophical approach with a tightly woven theoretical underpinning and a lengthy history of basic research in which B. F. Skinner was highly involved. But while the basic research continues, behavior analysis has gone on to demonstrate many important everyday applications to problems of individual, social and cultural significance.

Behavior analysis seems to be steadily growing in its influence, though at the time of Skinner's death in 1990 he was highly disappointed that his ideas had not had more impact. Presently, there are several organizations devoted to behavior analysis. The most visible of these is the Association for Behavior Analysis International which has its headquarters on the campus of Western Michigan University in Kalamazoo, Michigan. It has over 3,000 members and 30 affiliate organizations in various states and foreign countries including Ireland, Belgium, Great Britain, Germany, Italy, Japan, Norway, Peru, and Uruguay.

There are about two dozen journals presently in publication that are devoted to the theoretical, experimental, and applied analysis of behavior.

To find out more one may write to the Association for Behavior Analysis International, 213 West Hall, Western Michigan University, Kalamazoo, Michigan 49008-5052. Or one may call that organization at Area Code 616-387-8341 or Fax at Area Code 616-387-8354, or see its website at www.wmich.edu/aba.

Bourgeois, M.S. (1990). Enhancing conversation skills in patients with Alzheimer's disease using a prosthetic memory aid. *Journal of Applied Behavior Analysis*, 23, 29-42.

Grote, I., & Baer, D.M. (1991, May). *The Effects of Different Choices on Preschoolers' Self-Control.* Paper presented at the meeting of the Association for Behavior Analysis International, Atlanta.

B. F. Skinner From A to Z

A

Aggression

A given instance of aggression can generally be traced to both phylogenic and ontogenic contingencies, since both kinds of variables are generally operative upon a given occasion.[1] (p. 24)

Author note:

Here, as occurs often throughout Skinner's works, his reference is to the influences on behavior of both genetics and learning. "Phylogenic contingencies" is Skinner's term for what is inherited through the genetic structure, while "ontogenic contingencies" is his term for what is learned by a single individual in its lifetime. It is apropos that the first entry in this book addresses one of the frequent misconceptions about Skinner. That is, he is often misrepresented, even among scholars, as being a strict environmentalist who did not believe in genetic influences on behavior. Clearly, that is not the case.

The Arts

We might say...that it is the business of the entertainer, writer, artist, or musician to create reinforcing events.

W. Joseph Wyatt

In the process of creation...a medium may be manipulated to reveal self- reinforcing properties, but the "universality" of a work of art is measured by the number of other people who also find it reinforcing.[2] *(p. 315)*

Author Note:
Skinner was highly interested in the arts. He subjected the activity of artists to a theoretical behavioral analysis. He objected to explanations such as "He creates art because he has a great deal of creativity." Skinner found such explanations circular ("How do we know a person has creativity?" "Because he creates art.")

Attention
The attention of people is reinforcing because it is a necessary condition for other reinforcements from them. In general, only people who are attending to us reinforce our behavior.[2] *(p. 78).*

Author Note:
Skinner felt that our desire for attention is learned. He saw as superficial the often heard explanation that we are born with a need for attention.

Autonomous Man
What is being abolished by behavior analysis is autonomous man-the inner man, the homunculus, the possessing demon, the man defended by the literatures of freedom and dignity.

His abolition has long been overdue. Autonomous

man is a device used to explain what we cannot explain in any other way. He has been constructed from our ignorance, and as our understanding increases, the very stuff of which he is composed vanishes.[3] (p.191)

Author Note:

Throughout history explanations for otherwise unexplained behavior have simply been created by using our imaginations. For example, a person behaving oddly might historically have been said to be acting that way because he was possessed by a demon, or, more recently, because he is possessed by an "id" or by a "libido" or by some other unobserved entity which exactly explains the behavior in question. Skinner thought such explanations were fictions, simply made up on the spot, explaining nothing. One other such demon for Skinner is the "will."

To say that a person had the will to do a thing explains little or nothing according to Skinner. "Will" was just another version of the inner demon, or the inner angel, which in Skinner's analysis does not exist.

Awareness

We are aware of what we are doing when we describe the topography of our behavior. We are aware of why we are doing it when we describe relevant variables, such as important aspects of the occasion or the reinforcement.[1] (p. 244)

W. Joseph Wyatt

Author Note:

Skinner has been misperceived as ignoring conscious awareness or conscious experience. This mistake coincides with another misperception--that Skinner felt nothing important was happening inside the individual. As this quotation shows, Skinner was well aware that people think about what they are doing and why they are doing it.

B

Behavior as Subject Matter

It is rare to find behavior dealt with as a subject matter in its own right. Instead it is regarded as evidence for a mental life, which is then taken as the primary object of inquiry.[4] (p. 84)

Author Note:

What people do, including what they think and feel, is proper subject matter in a science of behavior, for Skinner. He deplored the tendency (in most of psychology) to neglect the study of what people do in favor of the study of inner mental life, which explained little.

Behaviorism

Behaviorism is not the science of human behavior; it is the philosophy of that science. Some of the questions it asks are these: Is such a science really possible? Can it account for every aspect of human behavior? What methods can it use? Are its laws as valid as those of physics and biology? Will it lead to a technology, and if so what role will it play in human affairs?[5] (p. 3)

Author Note:

Behaviorism is a philosophy. The science and applications that grow out of it are best referred to as behavior analysis.

W. Joseph Wyatt

Behavior Modification

Behavior modification is environment modification, but this is not widely recognized. Very little current "behavioral science" is really behavioral because prescientific modes of explanation still flourish, but behavior modification is an outstanding exception.[6] *(p. 280)*

Author Note:

Throughout the late 1960s and 1970s a proliferation of books and journals devoted to applications of behavior analysis occurred. As this quotation from 1972 indicates, Skinner was, perhaps, beginning to feel that his ideas were taking root.

Benevolence

The consequences responsible for benevolent, devoted, compassionate, or public-spirited behavior are forms of countercontrol, and when they are lacking, these much-admired features of behavior are lacking.[5] *(p. 210)*

Author Note:

We explain little or nothing, according to Skinner, by saying that a person does something good because he has the trait of benevolence or does something compassionate because he possesses the trait of compassion. Rather, kindly activity occurs because it is reinforced. The reinforcers might include everything from tax breaks, to approval from others in the community, to approval from one's self.

Blame

Although people object when a scientific analysis traces their behavior to external conditions and thus deprives them of credit and the chance to be admired, they seldom object when the same analysis absolves them of blame.[3] (p. 71)

Author Note:

We are personally responsible for little or none of our activity, be it good or bad. Yet we tend to be much more likely to accept praise for our good work, as if we were personally responsible for it, than to accept blame for our failures, in which case we tend to avoid the responsibility, if possible.

W. Joseph Wyatt

C

Classroom Discipline

The current nationwide problem of school discipline is frequently, though possibly erroneously, attributed to progressive education. Whatever its explanation, it is a serious problem. How can we recapture the orderly conduct once attributed to "discipline" without reinstating all the undesirable by-products of an inhumane aversive control? The answer is; use positive reinforcement instead of punishment.[7] *(p. 97)*

Author Note:

This was written in 1958. Skinner noticed that often the classroom disciplinary style of many teachers involves punishment for bad behavior rather than reinforcement for good behavior. Sadly, until his death in 1990 he felt that little had changed. Notwithstanding the myth that behavior analysis is usually punitive, this is one more instance in which Skinner's advocacy of positive methods over negative is clear.

Classroom Failure

By admitting that we cannot teach, we avoid confessing that we have failed to do so, and we thus continue to maintain, as teachers have maintained for centuries that it is always the student who fails, not the teacher.[8] *(p. 707)*

Author Note:

We tend to blame the student when learning does not occur. We say that the student is lazy, unmotivated, or the like. A system in which positive reinforcement energizes the student was Skinner's goal.

Clinical Psychology

A conception of human behavior based primarily on clinical information and practice will undoubtedly differ from a conception emanating from the laboratory. This does not mean that either is superior to the other, or that eventually a common formulation will not prove useful to both.[4] *(p. 81)*

Author Note:

Because Skinner was primarily an experimentalist, only occasionally delving into applications with humans, some have developed the impression that he was averse to, or rejected, clinical applications. This is a misconception sometimes found even among otherwise well trained behavior analysts. Little could be further from the truth. It was his dream that his laboratory findings would find their way to clinics where they would be used to enhance human potential.

Cognitive Science

Cognitive science is the creation science of psychology, as it struggles to maintain the position of a mind or self.[9] *(p. 1209)*

W. Joseph Wyatt

Author Note:

This statement was made during Skinner's acceptance speech at the presentation of his lifetime achievement award from the American Psychological Association only a week before his death. To the end Skinner remained convinced that psychology's return to cognitive formulations in the late 1970s and 1980s was counterproductive to the development of a science of behavior.

College Teaching

The most casual attitude toward a better under-standing of instruction is evident at all levels. You will not find anything like a medical school, law school, or business school for those who want to be college teachers. No professional training is felt to be necessary.[8] *(p. 704)*

Author Note:

If we desire that teachers, including college teachers, be good at their jobs then they will have to be trained to teach. Currently this is not the case for college professors. This is another instance in which Skinner was willing to be critical of his own profession.

Common Sense

The disastrous results of common sense in the management of human behavior are evident in every walk of life, from international affairs to the care of a baby, and we shall continue to be inept in all these fields until a scientific analysis clarifies the advantages of a more effective tech-

nology. It will then be obvious that the results are due to more than common sense.[5] (p. 258)

Author Note:
> Leaving important activities such as child care to "common sense" is a mistake in Skinner's view. To do so is to leave important tasks to be shaped by whatever accidental influences might bear upon them.

Conformity

Behavior comes to conform to the standards of a given community when certain responses are reinforced and others are allowed to go unreinforced or are punished.[2] (p. 415)

Author Note:
> We sometimes ask ourselves why a person conforms, particularly an individual whose conformance seems too rigid. Skinner believed that conformity was simply a class of behavior which occurred because it was reinforced, or because efforts to break free from it were punished by the disapproval of peers and others in the community.

Consequences

The consequences of behavior may "feed back" into the organism. When they do so, they may change the probability that the behavior which produced them will occur again. The English language contains many words, such as "reward" and "punishment," which refer to this effect, but we can get a clear picture of it only through

W. Joseph Wyatt

experimental analysis.[2] *(p. 59)*

Author Note:
Skinner devoted much of his life to studying the effects of positive and negative consequences on behavior. He frequently pointed out that one of the more interesting genetic influences on our behavior is that we can change it based on the consequences it generates.

Consciousness

Must we conclude that all those who have speculated about consciousness as a form of self-knowledge--from the Greeks to the British empiricists to the phenomenologists--have wasted their time? Perhaps we must. They deserve credit for directing attention to the relation between a person and his environment (the scientific study of stimulus control in the name of sensation and perception emerged from philosophical interests of that sort), but they have directed inquiry away from antecedent events in his environmental history.[5] *(p. 243)*

Author Note:
Skinner acknowledged the existence of conscience experience. He also held that it offered us little in the way of explanation of our behavior. He felt that looking inward for self-knowledge, a practice engaged in by the ancients and the modern day existential-phenomenologists, was not particularly useful. For example, to Skinner it is erroneous for a person to say that he rides a bicycle because he has

conscious knowledge of how to ride it. This ignores the actual reasons that the person is able to ride the bicycle--several hours of practice, coming under the influence of the pedals, wheels, gravity and the body's own balancing mechanisms.

Contingency of Reinforcement

An adequate formulation of the interaction between an organism and its environment must always specify three things: (1) the occasion upon which a response occurs, (2) the response itself, and (3) the reinforcing consequences. The interrelationships among them are the "contingencies of reinforcement."[1] (p. 7)

Author Note:

The "contingency of reinforcement" is one of the fundamental features of Skinner's behavioral science. The contingency has three parts: The first part is what happens before behavior occurs. The second part is the behavior itself. The third part is the consequence, that is, what comes after the behavior.

Consider what happens when a person asks you for the loan of a pen. First is a question, "May I borrow your pen?" Next is your behavior. You hand the person the pen. And the third part of a contingency of reinforcement is the consequence of what you did. The borrower smiles and politely says, "Thank you very much. I'll return it in a moment," and then does so. Your response (handing over the pen) to an initial stimulus (the

W. Joseph Wyatt

request) was reinforced by a pleasant consequence, making you more likely to repeat the loan in a later similar circumstance. Note, though, that a negative consequence (if, for example, the pen had not been returned) would reduce the probability of your loaning the pen again, at least to the same person.

Control of Human Behavior

We must surely begin with the fact that human behavior is always controlled. "Man is born free," said Rousseau, "and is everywhere in chains," but no one is less free than a newborn child, nor will he become free as he grows older. His only hope is that he will come under the control of a natural and social environment in which he will make the most of genetic endowment and in doing so most successfully pursue happiness.[5] (p. 221)

Author Note:

There have been no more strident criticisms of behavior analysis than its rejection of free will and its adoption of the view that all behavior is determined. Skinner believed that the individual who tells himself that he is free to do as he wishes is simply engaging in a self-deception. The most free we can be, according to Skinner, is to understand the variables that control us.

Creativity

The key word in Darwin's title was "origin." Natural selection explained the origination of millions of different species on the surface of the earth, without appealing to a creative mind. In the field of human behavior the possibility arises that contingencies of reinforcement may explain a work of art or the solution to a problem in mathematics or science without appealing to a different kind of creative mind or to a trait of creativity...[5] (p. 246-7)

Author Note:

To say that a person solves a problem in math or produces a work of art because he possesses a trait known as "creativity" is circular and explains nothing in Skinner's view. This is because, if asked how we know the creativity is present in the individual, we are left saying little except that we have observed the individual solving the problem or producing the artistic work.

Not only is this a mistake, according to Skinner it clouds our inquiry into the real causes of problem solving or artistic creation. A behavioral analysis is the way that we will understand the real processes involved. Then we will be able to create more art, and develop increasingly clever solutions to mathematical or scientific problems.

D

Democracy

Democracy is a version of countercontrol designed to solve the problem of manipulation.[5] *(p. 267)*

Author Note:

Little was left out of Skinner's analysis, including democracy. It is an irony that Skinner was occasionally accused of advocating a totalitarian government because, in fact, he viewed totalitarianism as destructive and felt that creation of democracy is a natural response by people because they prefer positive systems of control.

Dignity

Any evidence that a person's behavior may be attributed to external circumstances seems to threaten his dignity or worth. We are not inclined to give a person credit for achievements which are in fact due to forces over which he has no control. We tolerate a certain amount of such evidence, as we accept without alarm some evidence that a man is not free. No one is greatly disturbed when important details of works of art and literature, political careers, and scientific discoveries are attributed to "influences" in the lives of artists, writers, statesmen, and scientists respectively. But as an analysis of behavior adds further evidence, the achievements for which a person himself is to be given credit seem to approach zero, and both the evidence and the science which produces it are then challenged.³ (p. 41)

Author Note:

Through the second half of the 20th Century it became evident to Skinner that science was explaining more activity that previously was credited to a person's motivation, willpower, etc. Some individuals disapproved of his analysis because they felt robbed of their dignity if they could not take credit for their achievements, though they were less concerned about their dignity when forced to take credit for their failures. (Most of the time they were willing to forego references to their dignity in order to forego blame for their failures.) Ultimately Skinner and other behavior analysts began to recognize that the most dignified position a person may achieve is to truly understand the forces, both good and bad, that influence his behavior.

W. Joseph Wyatt

E

Economics

...economics is perhaps the first field in which an explicit change was made to positive reinforcement. Most men now work, as we say, "for the money".[1] (p. 18)

Author Note:

Economics was an area of major interest to Skinner. He realized that there had been gradual change over the years from punitive methods of controlling work among the masses to more positive methods. The Pharaohs got the pyramids built but the slaves who did the building did so primarily to avoid the sting of the whip. As centuries passed a more productive method evolved in most parts of the world. It is positive reinforcement. We work for the money, and in some happy instances, for the intrinsic rewards of our work as well.

Education (1)

...we are on the verge of a new educational "method"--a new pedagogy--in which the teacher will emerge as a skilled behavioral engineer. He will be able to analyze the contingencies which arise in his classes, and design and set up improved versions. He will know what is to be done and will have the satisfaction of knowing that he has done it.[10] (p. 99)

Author Note:

At times Skinner has been accused of attempting to do away with teachers entirely, replacing them with machines. However, a reading of his work makes it clear that Skinner had no such plan. Instead, he advocated that teachers adopt behavioral methods, particularly the use of reinforcement for correct schoolwork. In fact, this is now the method of choice in many classrooms throughout the United States and other parts of the world.

Education (2)

Everyone has suffered, and unfortunately is continuing to suffer, from mentalistic theories of learning in education. It is a field in which the goal seems to be obviously a matter of changing minds, attitudes, feelings, motives, and so on, and the Establishment is therefore particularly resistant to change. Yet the point of education can be stated in behavioral terms: a teacher arranges contingencies under which the student acquires behavior which will be useful to him under other contingencies later on. The instructional contingencies must be contrived; there is no way out of this. The teacher cannot bring enough of the real life of the student into the classroom to build behavior appropriate to the contingencies he will encounter later. The behaviors to be constructed in advance are as much a matter of productive thinking and creativity as of plain facts and skills.[5] (p. 202-3)

Author Note:

Skinner deplored intrusion into classrooms of what he called "mentalistic" theories of education. He objected to theories in which the goal was something other than teaching children to read better, to do arithmetic more quickly and accurately and the like. Skinner was much in favor of the three Rs as goals for learning in classrooms.

But he didn't stop there. He also understood that, for the most part, a child in school cannot appreciate the importance of education. That is, the school child has no way of coming in contact with either the real world problems that arise when one lacks adequate education, or the benefits should one become fairly well educated. Thus, Skinner believed that teachers were left with arranging "contingencies" which would result in optimal learning. Rather than telling a child "You'll be sorry 15 years from now if you don't have a good education," Skinner believed it most effective to provide the child with rewards or reinforcers for learning while still in the classroom.

Education (3)

...the educational institution cannot be content merely with establishing standard repertoires of right answers but must also establish a repertoire with which the student may, so to speak, arrive at the right answer under novel circumstances in the absence of any representative of the agency.[2] (p. 411)

Author Note:

Skinner responded to critics who complained that his methods would teach children to get the right answers but would not teach them to "think." His critics feared that students would be lost when in new situations, out of school, where circumstances were different than they had been in the classroom. Contrary to those criticisms, Skinner believed that responding under novel circumstances was itself a class of behavior which could be taught.

Emotion

Emotions Are Not Causes... As long as we conceive of the problem of emotion as one of inner states, we are not likely to advance a practical technology. It does not help in the solution of a practical problem to be told that some feature of a man's behavior is due to frustration or anxiety; we also need to be told how the frustration or anxiety has been induced and how it may be altered. [2] *(p. 167)*

Author Note:

Behavior analysts such as Skinner are frequently accused of ignoring, or denying the existence of, emotions. Clearly this was not true for Skinner, nor is it true of contemporary behavior analysts. Rather, behavior analysts believe that emotions have relatively little *causal* status.

It is wrong to attempt to explain, for example, a fistfight by saying, "Anger caused it," and it is a mistake to explain a hug by saying, "It was the result of joy." The reason such explanations are wrong is that we are still left to explain the origins of the anger and joy. Skinner had no interest in denying the existence of emotions, he only reinterpreted their causal role as of minimal importance in the explanation of behavior.

Epistemology

Students who are "competent in first-year college physics," for example, obviously differ from those who are not--but in what way? Even a tentative answer to that question should clarify the problem of teaching physics. It may well do more. In the not-too-distant future much more general issues in epistemology may be approached from the same direction. It is possible that we shall fully understand the nature of knowledge only after having solved the practical problems of imparting it.[11] (p. 391)

Author Note:

Epistemology is the study of how and why we know things. Skinner was keenly interested in epistemology and took a very practical approach to it. He believed that by being able to teach a student quickly, fluidly, and competently, we would best begin to understand the "nature of knowledge."

Ethics and Morals (1)

Almost everyone makes ethical and moral judgments but this does not mean that the human species has "an inborn need or demand for ethical standards." (We could say as well that we have an inborn need or demand for unethical behavior, since almost everyone behaves unethically at some time or other.) Man has not evolved as an ethical or moral animal. He has evolved to the point at which he has constructed an ethical or moral culture. He differs from the other animals not in possessing a moral or ethical sense but in having been able to generate a moral or ethical social environment.[3] (p. 167)

Author Note:

Humans are born neither noble nor ignoble. Nor are they born with any special tendency toward ethical or moral behavior. Because Skinner took this approach some have wrongly assumed that he felt that concepts such as ethics and morals are meaningless. A reading of Skinner shows that ethics and morals, in his view, arise not from within people but from within their cultures. The social environment tends to reward ethical and moral behavior and punish the unethical, at least in many instances (although at times the reverse happens-- leading to a great deal of unethical activity as well).

Ethics and Morals (2)

Man has been said to be superior to the other animals because he has evolved a moral or ethical sense... But what has evolved is a social environment in which individuals behave in ways determined in part by their effects on others. Different people show different amounts and kinds of moral and ethical behavior, depending upon the extent of their exposure to such contingencies. Morals and ethics have been said to involve "attitudes toward law and government which have taken centuries in the building," but it is much more plausible to say that the behavior said to express such attitudes is generated by contingencies that have developed over the centuries.[5] (p. 214-215)

W. Joseph Wyatt

Author Note:

Ethics and Morals exist in the reinforcement and punishment practices of our cultures, not in ourselves. To understand this makes us capable of generating further cultural practices which will strengthen and maintain ethical and moral activity among individuals. To not know or acknowledge the true origins of ethics and morals leaves us less ethical, less moral.

Existentialism

Existentialists, phenomenologists, and structuralists frequently contend that, in limiting itself to prediction and control, a science of behavior fails to grasp the essential nature or being of man...(but) The more thoroughly we understand the relation between human behavior and its genetic and environmental antecedents, the more clearly we understand the nature or essence of the species.[5] (p. 248-9)

Author Note:

Having been frequently criticized by philosophers within schools of thought such as existentialism, phenomenology, humanism, psychoanalysis, and structuralism, whose primary belief is that we can best understand the important and essential features of mankind by looking inward, Skinner defended his principles. He believed that we can best understand what is essential about humans by knowing what causes them to do the things they do. And these causes lie in their genes and in their environments.

Experimental Analysis of Behavior (1)

The experimental analysis of behavior is a rigorous, extensive, and rapidly advancing branch of biology, and only those who are unaware of its scope can call it oversimplified.[5] (p. 255)

Author Note:
Skinner answered those who dismissed his science as oversimplified. He viewed it as a branch of biology and felt that it was much more rigorous than most branches of psychology.

Experimental Analysis of Behavior (2)

...as we might expect, scientific analysis gives birth to technology. The insight into human behavior gained from research of this sort has already proved effective in many areas. The application to personnel problems in industry, to psychotherapy, to "human relations" in general, is clear. The most exciting technological extension at the moment appears to be in the field of education. The principles emerging from this analysis, and from a study of verbal behavior based upon it, are already being applied in the design of mechanical devices to facilitate instruction in reading, spelling, and arithmetic in young children, and routine teaching at the college level.

In the long run one may envisage a fundamental change in government itself, taking that term in the broadest possible sense. For a long time men of good will have tried to improve the cultural patterns in which they live. It is possible that a scientific analysis of behavior will provide us at last with the techniques we need for this task--with the wisdom we need to build a better world and, through it, better men.[12] *(p. 371)*

Author Note:

This comes from a paper written in 1957, when Skinner was in the middle of his career. He had seen some of his ideas come to be used in various settings, particularly education and in business and industry. He was encouraged but felt the progress had not gone far enough. It was his abiding view that his science, the experimental analysis of behavior, (today commonly referred to as behavior analysis), held the key that would unlock the door to a better world.

Explanatory Fiction

The best way to dispose of any explanatory fiction is to examine the facts upon which it is based. These usually prove to be, or suggest, variables which are acceptable from the point of view of scientific method.[2] *(p. 285)*

Author Note:

Throughout history there have been many fictional explanations of behavior. These explanations were readily accepted by the populous, and many of them have been generated by the professional psychological community.

For example to say that someone has a "need" to accomplish things, or the "ability" to read, or a "drive" to do a thing, is fictional and explains nothing. Behavior "explained" by terms such as need, ability, or drive could probably be traced to reinforcers, or instructions, or models showing how to do the activity, and these are the real causes of the behavior.

F

Feelings (1)

A behavioristic reformulation does not ignore feelings; it merely shifts the emphasis from the feeling to what is felt. A person responds to the physical world around him and, with a rather different set of nerves, to the no less physical world within his skin...

He does not take a particular street because he feels it is right; he feels it is right because he is inclined to take it, and he is so inclined because he has been reinforced for doing so. Similarly, in dealing with other people he feels that he is or is not doing the right thing, but he does not do it because he feels it is right; he feels it is right because it is what he tends to do, and he tends to do it because it has had consequences which were reinforcing first to others and then in turn to him. [13] *(p. 284)*

Author Note:

Skinner's analysis of what happens inside people was and is frequently misunderstood. He did not ignore feelings. Nor did he believe that feelings are nonexistent. Rather, Skinner felt that feelings are, simply, private behavior not directly observable to anyone else.

He believed that feelings are subject to the laws (reinforcement, punishment, stimulus control, etc.) that govern other behavior. But because feelings often accompany observable behavior they are often wrongly given credit for causing it. In fact, in a behavioral analysis, feelings are similar to observable behavior because both are caused by other variables, environmental and genetic.

Thus to say, "I went to the basketball game because I felt like it," would explain nothing. The real reasons for going to the game include what has happened previously at games (enjoyment) combined with other variables such as what one has learned about the potential for this game to be enjoyable. A more accurate statement would be, "I felt like I felt previously when attending other great games." In this analysis feelings accompany "going to the game," but do not cause it.

Feelings (2)

What is felt is certainly relevant to a causal sequence, but it does not follow that the act of feeling is an essential part of that sequence...

It is sometimes argued that we must mention the feelings in order to give an adequate description of the behavior, but what we need to mention are the controlling variables--which also account for the feelings.[1] (p. 256-7)

Author Note:

Skinner was interested in behaviorally analyzing feelings, though he viewed it as a difficult task, more difficult than analyzing observable behavior. Skinner clearly believed that feelings are an important part of existence, and he never denied their existence, as some have erroneously claimed.

W. Joseph Wyatt

Freedom

The feeling of freedom becomes an unreliable guide to action as soon as would-be controllers turn to nonaversive measures, as they are likely to do to avoid the problems raised when the controllee escapes or attacks. Nonaversive measures are not as conspicuous as aversive and are likely to be acquired more slowly, but they have obvious advantages which promote their use...

Until recently teaching was almost entirely aversive; the student studied to escape the consequences of not studying, but nonaversive techniques are gradually being discovered and used. The skillful parent learns to reward a child for good behavior rather than punish him for bad. Religious agencies move from the threat of hellfire to an emphasis on God's love, and governments turn from aversive sanctions to various kinds of inducements...

The effects are not as easily recognized as those of aversive contingencies because they tend to be deferred...but techniques as powerful as the older aversive techniques are now available.[3] (p. 30-31)

Author Note:

We are always controlled by our present circumstances combined with our genetic and environmental histories. When we feel that we do things freely it is more likely that we are simply free from aversive forms of control (punishment).

Moreover, negative methods of control often come back to haunt the controller when the one who is controlled fights back. Conversely, positive means of control are generally welcomed by the person who is controlled. Consider, for example, the treats given to hard working school children, the pay checks given to working adults, or the promise of heavenly rewards by a cleric to parishioners. Skinner recognized that these methods may act somewhat more slowly than punishment but are potentially more long lasting and powerful.

To stick to our traditional belief that we do things freely or by "choice" is to delude ourselves. Our behavior is always controlled, even if positively.

Free Will

Prevailing philosophies of human nature recognize an internal "will" which has the power of interfering with causal relationships and which makes the prediction and control of behavior impossible. To suggest that we abandon this view is to threaten many cherished beliefs...

Primitive beliefs about man and his place in nature are usually flattering. It has been the unfortunate responsibility of science to paint more realistic pictures. [2] *(p. 7)*

Author Note:

Skinner, like Freud, and many behavioral scientists, rejected the notion of free will. To Skinner "free will" was fiction and was an easy way to seem to "explain" behavior.

Yet, Skinner noted that people cling very strongly to the idea that they possess free will. He hypothesized that is so because it is flattering. In this quotation we see a note of discouragement in Skinner's tone as he makes it clear that, as a behavioral scientist, he has felt it necessary to,

W. Joseph Wyatt

"paint a more realistic picture."

Functional Analysis

Implicit in a functional analysis is the notion of control...Proving the validity of a functional relation by an actual demonstration of the effect of one variable upon another is the heart of experimental science. The practice enables us to dispense with many troublesome statistical techniques in testing the importance of variables.[2] *(p. 227)*

Author Note:

Skinner was a psychologist by training, experience, and practice at the laboratory level. But he was unhappy with traditional psychological methods that use large groups of subjects, find the mean score on some variable for those subjects, and then compare it to some other large group of subjects who had some different form of treatment. If a large enough difference is found between the average scores for each group then "statistical significance" is found.

However, for Skinner this does not answer the question of how to get an individual subject to do a thing reliably under controlled laboratory conditions. It is not enough to know that the average of one group is different from the average of another group.

Thus, Skinner developed the functional analysis. As an example consider a teacher who seeks help for a problem student. The teacher might be instructed to pay attention to the student only when the student is behaving well. Over time it might be observed that the student begins to demonstrate more and more good behavior, less and less inappropriate behavior. Then the teacher is instructed to reverse the procedures, paying attention to bad behavior and ignoring the good. The child then begins to engage in more and more unacceptable behavior. Finally to put the classroom back in order and to further demonstrate the experimental control that had been established, the teacher is once again instructed to pay attention only to the good behavior. This is what is meant by a functional analysis in its simplest form. Experimental control has been demonstrated over an individual subject.

W. Joseph Wyatt

G

Genetics

Operant conditioning is as much a part of the genetic endowment as digestion or gestation. The question is not whether the human species has a genetic endowment but how it is to be analyzed. It begins and remains a biological system, and the behavioristic position is that it is nothing more than that...

One unfortunate consequence is that genetic sources sometimes become a kind of dumping ground: any aspect of behavior which at the moment escapes analysis in terms of contingencies of reinforcement is likely to be assigned to genetic endowment, and we are likely to accept the explanation because we are so accustomed to going no further than a state of the organism.[5] (p. 48-49)

Author Note:

Although it was not his specialty, Skinner possessed a great deal of respect for the study of genetics. He recognized that genes are an important part of our endowment and that genetics would ultimately explain some important aspects of human behavior. He regretted, though, that genetics was often used as a kind of explanatory catch-all. That is, he noticed a tendency in the behavioral sciences community for any behavior that needed explanation to be attributed to a person's genetic endowment, whether or not that had been demonstrated via research.

Government (1)

Government has always been the special field of aversive control.[14] *(p. 1061)*

Author Note:

Governments historically have used aversive means of control. Consider that laws are typically written to indicate what "thou shalt not" do. And the government punishes individuals who violate the law.

Is it possible to have a government that controls people positively? Skinner believed so. For example, the use of a lottery, which amounts to a voluntary tax, is a method by which the government may accumulate income less aversively than simply by taxing one's income or handing out speeding tickets.

Government (2)

Under a government which controls through positive reinforcement the citizen feels free, though he is no less controlled. Freedom from government is freedom from aversive consequences. We choose a form of government which maximizes freedom for a very simple reason: aversive events are aversive. A government which makes the least use of its power to punish is most likely to reinforce our behavior in supporting it.[2] *(p. 348)*

W. Joseph Wyatt

Author Note:

Skinner felt that democratic forms of government tend to survive because they are less aversive than other forms. When he wrote, "We choose a form of government which maximizes freedom..." he meant freedom from aversive forms of control.

Always, though, it was foremost in Skinner's thinking that even positive forms of control are just that--control. He did not mean to imply that we may act completely freely, only that we may act free from negative means of control.

H

Happiness

Happiness is a feeling, a by-product of operant reinforcement. The things which make us happy are the things which reinforce us, but it is the things, not the feelings, which must be identified and used in prediction, control, and interpretation.[5] (p. 78)

Author Note:

A person does not do a thing because he feels happy. Rather, he feels happy because he has done something that has been reinforced. To understand happiness we must look outside the individual to identify the things that created the happiness, rather than inside the individual in a fruitless effort to understand more about the feeling of happiness itself.

Heaven and Hell

Traditional descriptions of Heaven and Hell epitomize positive and negative reinforcement...The power achieved by the religious agency depends upon how effectively certain verbal reinforcements are conditioned--in particular the promise of Heaven and the threat of Hell...

In actual practice a threat to bar from Heaven or to consign to Hell is made contingent upon sinful behavior, while virtuous behavior brings a promise of Heaven or a release from the threat of Hell.[2] (p. 352-53)

W. Joseph Wyatt

Author Note:

As with government, education, and other large scale systems of control, Skinner was quite interested in religion. He felt there was a direct correspondence between the influence of a religion and its ability to condition or teach people that their behavior would result in an eventual trip to either Heaven or Hell.

Heroes

We may mourn the passing of heroes but not the conditions which make for heroism.[15] *(p. 61)*

Author Note:

The heroic act is as much a product of an individual's environmental and genetic histories as any other activity and, thus, is not essentially different from any other act. Perhaps a better understanding of behavior will lead us ultimately to conditions where heroes are no longer needed. Eventual elimination of conditions that lead to war provides us with an example. No more war--and no more war heroes.

Higher Mental Processes

Human beings attend to or disregard the world in which they live. They search for things in that world. They generalize from one thing to another. They discriminate. They respond to single features or special sets of features as "abstractions" or "concepts." They solve problems by assembling, classifying, arranging and rearranging things.

They describe things and respond to their descriptions, as well as to descriptions made by others. They analyze the contingencies of reinforcement in their world and extract plans and rules which enable them to respond appropriately without direct exposure to the contingencies. They discover and use rules for deriving new rules from old. In all this, and much more, they are simply behaving, and that is true even when they are behaving covertly. Not only does a behavioral analysis not reject any of these higher mental processes; it has taken the lead in investigating the contingencies under which they occur. What it rejects is the assumption that comparable activities take place in the mysterious world of the mind. That assumption, it argues, is an unwarranted and dangerous metaphor...

No matter how defective a behavioral account may be, we must remember that mentalistic explanations explain nothing.[5] (p. 245-6)

Author Note:

Some of Skinner's harshest criticism has come from other behavioral scientists who wrongly believe that Skinner disavowed the existence of thinking and other internal activities. Skinner had heard this complaint so often that by the time he wrote this in 1974 he was weary from hearing it.

What he rejected was the infusion of unscientific assumptions and terms (often borrowed from the lay population) which explained little or nothing about important processes such as thinking. Consider cognitive psychology's metaphor of storage and retrieval of memory. Skinner believed that when the cognitivists said that a person did something because

W. Joseph Wyatt

he "remembered" how to do it, or because he had "information about it stored in long-term memory," that nothing was explained. To Skinner this was mentalism and was no better than attributing the activity to a person's will, his actualization potential, his "need" to do it, his drive to do it, his ability to do it, to his libido, or to a demon which had gotten into his body and caused him to do it.

Humanistic Psychology

So-called humanistic psychologists control people if they have any effect at all, but they do not allow themselves to analyze their practices. One unfortunate result is that they cannot teach them--and may even say that teaching is wrong.[5] *(p. 205)*

Author Note:

Humanistic psychology attempted to do the impossible when it attempted to develop therapeutic practices that were uncontrolling and nondirective.

Consider the task of the humanistic therapist who is taking a nondirective approach to his client. If the nondirective therapist can get predictable results, such as increased self-awareness, in his client, then, paradoxically, the therapist has abandoned his effort to remain nondirective by exerting control over the client, in Skinner's view.

I

Individuality

The individual is at best a locus in which many lines of development come together in a unique set. His individuality is unquestioned. Every cell in his body is a unique genetic product, as unique as that classic mark of individuality, the fingerprint. And even within the most regimented culture every personal history is unique.[3] (p. 200)

Author Note:

One of the most perplexing, though often heard, criticisms is that Skinner ignored the individuality of the person. That lies in direct contrast to another of the criticisms--that he too frequently used individual subjects (as opposed to large groups) in his research.

It is clear that Skinner recognized the uniqueness of individuals. He simply did not give them personal credit for their accomplishments (nor personal blame for their failures) because he felt that the person was best conceptualized as a place or "locus" in which his genetic and environmental histories uniquely came together to produce a given behavior.

Insight

Awareness may help if the problem is in part a lack of awareness, and "insight" into one's condition may help if one then takes remedial action, but awareness or insight alone is not always enough, and it may be too much. One need not be aware of one's behavior or the conditions controlling it in order to behave effectively--or ineffectively.[3] *(p. 183)*

Author Note:

Traditional psychoanalytic therapy involved the notion that insight was necessary in order to solve one's problems therapeutically. Insight typically involved becoming aware of one's unconscious conflicts.

Skinner challenged that directly. He believed that we all do many things despite the fact that we are unaware of (lack insight into) their causes. However, Skinner refused to place those causes in the unconscious part of the mind, preferring to locate the causes of our actions in our genetic and environmental histories. Skinner also recognized that simply being aware of the causes of our mal-adaptive behaviors was no guarantee that we could change them.

Introspection

In some theories of knowledge, introspective observations may be regarded as primary data, but in an analysis of behavior they are a form of theorizing which is not required or necessarily helpful.[16] *(p. 510)*

Author Note:

Introspection was the first formal psychological method, having been developed by Wilhelm Wundt in Leipzig, Germany in the late 1800s. Recent theories, particularly those of the phenomenologists, have traded on this history by holding that we can learn the most important things about ourselves by looking inward.

Skinner did not reject the fact that important things happen inside of people. Rather, he objected to the idea that the *most* important things about us can be found by looking inward. The causes of what we do, think and feel can best be determined by looking outward to our environments, in most cases.

Intuition

Behaving intuitively, in the sense of behaving as the effect of unanalyzed contingencies, is the very starting point of a behavioristic analysis. A person is said to behave intuitively when he does not use reason. Instinct is sometimes a synonym: it is said to be a mistake to "attribute to logical design what is the result of blind instinct," but the reference is simply to behavior shaped by unanalyzed contingencies of reinforcement.[5] (p. 146)

Author Note:

For behavior analysts there is a cause for everything that an organism does, be it a person or a subhuman species. We do not explain anything that a person does by attributing it to "intuition" or to "instinct." When we use such terms we are admitting that we simply do not know the actual causes of the behavior.

W. Joseph Wyatt

J

Joy and Sorrow

Some emotions--joy and sorrow, for example--involve the whole repertoire of the organism. We recognize this when we say that an emotion is exciting or depressing.[2] (p. 163)

Author Note:

This quotation, which was written in 1953, demonstrates that Skinner recognized the importance of emotions. At the same time, its rather dry tone may suggest why some have accused Skinner of denying the existence of emotions or at least downplaying their importance.

In fact Skinner downplayed their importance only with respect to their supposed status as causes of behavior.

Judeo-Christian Tradition

The religious communities in the Judeo-Christian tradition were based on sets of rules (e.g. the Rules of Benedict and Augustine) specifying contingencies of social reinforcement.[17] (p.21)

Author Note:

The control of people by religious guidelines and rules, such as The Ten Commandments, was of lifelong interest to Skinner. He conceptualized such "commandments" as contingencies of reinforcement. For example, "Thou shalt not kill" (implying eternal damnation if you do) specifies a punitive contingency. "Love thy neighbor as thyself," specifies a positive contingency, implying one will receive love in return.

Jung, Carl

Jung's archetypal patterns and collective unconscious can be traced to either the evolution of the species or the evolution of cultural practices. "The astonishing sameness of the repressed unconscious across all recorded eras and civilizations," is the sameness of the things which reinforce people and of the behaviors which prove injurious to others.[5] (p. 167)

Author Note:

It is occasionally said that Skinner paid little attention to the work of other great thinkers in the field. However, a careful reading of his work makes it clear that he was very much aware of what had been and continued to be written by others.

This example shows that he acknowledged the theorizing of psychoanalyst Carl Jung who postulated that all people carry the same powerful primordial forces in their unconscious minds and that these account for the similarities of broad behavior patterns (such as prohibitions against incest, belief in a deity, etc.) in people across cultures. Skinner reformulated the causes in behavior analytic terms. He saw the broad similarities among

W. Joseph Wyatt

peoples as the result of the fact that people,
regardless of culture, have many of the same
reinforcers (food, clothing, shelter, strength in
numbers when fighting enemies, etc.).

K

Knowing

There is room in a behavioristic analysis for a kind of knowing short of action and hence short of power. One need not be actively behaving in order to feel or to introspectively observe certain states normally associated with behavior. To say, "I know a sea lion when I see one," is to report that one can identify a sea lion but not that one is now doing so.[5] (p. 154)

Author Note:

The study of knowledge and knowing was of enormous interest to Skinner. It was an area that fascinated him throughout his career and he seemed never to tire of its study.

It is ironic that some have erroneously written that Skinner put little emphasis on knowing, or that he denied the existence of the phenomenon of knowing.

While Skinner objected to cavalier use of the term "know," he recognized readily that people can know things and he operationally defined what that means. He frowned on "explanations" that attributed our behavior to "knowledge." For example, a child does not do math because he "knows" how. That statement explains nothing, in Skinner's view. The child's math performance would be better explained by looking at the teaching, training, and practice that the child underwent. No doubt these would include the instructions given by the teacher, models of sample problems provided by the teacher, consequences such as praise from the teacher, etc. These were the real explanations, according to Skinner.

Knowledge

We say that a newborn baby knows how to cry, suckle, and sneeze. We say that a child knows how to walk and how to ride a tricycle. The evidence is simply that the baby and child exhibit the behavior specified. Moving from verb to noun, we say that they possess behavior. It is in this sense that we say that people thirst for, pursue, and acquire knowledge.

But this brings us at once to the question of what it means to possess behavior...to say that a response is emitted does not imply that it has been inside the organism. Behavior exists only when it being executed.[5] (p. 151)

Author Note:

In his later years Skinner devoted considerable time to what he felt were serious errors in the "cognitive science" that had become popular in psychology in the 1970s and 1980s. He especially objected to the cognitive metaphor of acquiring information and storing it in either short-term or long-term memory.

We do not store small samples of behavior inside us which we then let out when the occasion is appropriate (or sometimes inappropriate), according to Skinner. In his view behavior is something that we do, contrary to the cognitive science metaphor which tells us that it is something which we possess inside us in "storage" like files in a cabinet or information in a computer.

(Self-)Knowledge

Self-knowledge is of social origin. It is only when a person's private world becomes important to others that it is made important to him... A behavioristic analysis does not question the practical usefulness of reports of the inner world that is felt and introspectively observed... Nevertheless, the private world within the skin is not clearly observed or known.[5] *(p. 35)*

Author Note:

Knowing one's "self" can best be done by knowing the environmental and genetic factors which control one's behavior. Those who believe that self-knowledge is greatest when we look inward, or introspect, are wrong, in the behavior analytic view.

But contrary to a frequently seen misrepresentation in the psychological literature, this in no way implied that Skinner viewed people as "empty organisms" in which nothing important goes on inside.

W. Joseph Wyatt

L

Language Development

We have noted that those who study the "development of language" in the child tell us much about vocabulary, grammar, and length of sentences but very little about the hundreds of thousands of occasions upon which a child hears words and sentences spoken or the many thousands of times he himself speaks them with results, and that no adequate account of the "development of language" is therefore possible.[5] (p. 128)

Author Note:

Language development should be studied in the same way as the development of any other complex behavior. Skinner recognized that language is extremely difficult to study because of its complexity but saw that difficulty as a problem ultimately to be solved through a behavioral analysis.

Language develops because over a period of several years the young child makes tens of thousands of efforts to produce sound (verbal behavior) and its verbal community has an equal number of opportunities to reinforce, ignore, or even punish each of those instances. Those are the primary factors which create language. It is a mistake to think that people have inside them genetically inherited rules of grammar that shape their acquisition of language.

Law

A law usually has two important features. In the first place, it specifies behavior...In the second place, a law specifies or implies a consequence, usually punishment. A law is thus a statement of a contingency of reinforcement maintained by a governmental agency.[2] *(p. 339)*

Author Note:
Laws are best thought of as statements of contingencies of reinforcement. That is, a behavior is specified and the result of doing it is made clear.

Lawfulness of Behavior

In our present state of knowledge, certain events therefore appear to be unpredictable. It does not follow that these events are free or capricious. Since human behavior is enormously complex and the human organism is of limited dimensions, many acts may involve processes to which the Principle of Indeterminacy applies. It does not follow that human behavior is free, but only that it may be beyond the range of a predictive or controlling science.[2] *(p. 17)*

Author Note:
The fact that behavioral science has not progressed to the point where everything a person does can be accurately predicted and controlled should not be taken as evidence that these activities are done freely, or without control.

A line from a Broadway musical said, "Everything's up to date in Kansas City. They've gone about as far as they can go." The foolishness of the belief that behavioral science has gone as far as it can go should be self-evident. It would be equally wrong to think that behavior which is up to now unexplained must be due to free will or caprice and could not possibly have been caused by a set of potentially understandable variables.

Perhaps Skinner's most fundamental assumption, from which all else in his research and theory flowed, was simply that behavior is lawful.

Love

The statement "I love my wife" seems to be a report of feelings, but it also involves a probability of action...With respect to a person with whom we interact, then, to "love" is to behave in ways having certain kinds of effects, possibly with accompanying conditions which may be felt. [5] *(p. 54)*

Author Note:

There is a disadvantage to being a behavioral scientist who attempts to explain important phenomena such as love. This statement by Skinner is stilted and formal, and a bit humorous. Yet, because Skinner and other behavior analysts were willing to bear the burden of behaviorally analyzing love, whole cultures may benefit by ultimately being able to produce more of it.

Skinner is frequently misrepresented as disavowing the existence of important internal events such as feelings of love. This statement makes it clear that such is not the case. Rather, Skinner simply attempted to carefully define love as involving both a feeling and a probability of observable action.

Lower Animals, Study of

Another common misunderstanding concerns extrapolation from animal to human behavior. Those who study living organisms--say, in genetics, embryology, or medicine--usually start below the human level, and students of behavior have quite naturally followed the same practice...

It is frequently implied that human dignity is threatened when principles derived from the study of lower animals are applied to man; but if we really believe that the proper study of mankind is man, we must not reject any relevant information.[1] (p.100-1)

Author Note:

Skinner was the target of occasional criticism because of his efforts to show that some of the general principles of learning for lower animals are the same for humans. Despite the criticisms he persisted. There is no longer any question among thoughtful behavioral scientists as to the validity of his claims.

The results continue to better the condition of mankind in many areas. For example, shaping, in which small approximations to a goal behavior are reinforced, has greatly elevated the humanity of the living conditions of severely and profoundly retarded individuals. Low functioning people now are able to be trained to be independent in much of their self care.

W. Joseph Wyatt

Despite such advances there are still those who complain that Skinner's work with lower animals, and application of that work to humans, somehow robs people of their dignity. Skinner is in good company. Charles Darwin received the same kind of criticism when he suggested that humans shared other features with lower species.

M

Man, the machine

Man is a machine, but he is a very complex one. At present he is far beyond the powers of men to construct--except, of course, in the usual biological way. Only those who believe that something nonphysical is essential to his functioning are likely to question this. If a science of human behavior is impossible because man possesses free will, or if behavior cannot be explained without invoking a miracle-working mind, then indeed man cannot be simulated.[18] (p. 294-5)

Author Note:

Most of us were taught in elementary school health classes that the human body is a marvelous machine. We did not recoil at that knowledge, given that it seemed reasonable, it was told to us by authority figures, and there was no major literature against it.

But in those same classes, and perhaps in others such as history or civics or government classes, we were taught something quite different with respect to behavior. There we were taught, wrongly in Skinner's view, that our behavior is due to a host of metaphysical factors lurking inside us--free will being the most commonly mentioned. In fact, the concept of free will is one of the major building blocks of our western democratic society.

That is one reason why Skinner's theory is so

frequently and virulently attacked. Skinner believed that all behavior can ultimately be explained without references to "will" or other nonphysical entities that are outside the realm of matter and energy with which a natural science deals.

Marriage

Marriage is often described as a system in which unlimited sexual contact with a selected partner is contingent on nonsexual behavior useful to the culture--such as supporting and managing a household and family and, following St. Paul's famous principle, forsaking sexual activity elsewhere.[19] *(p. 164)*

Author Note:

Here, with a touch of humor, Skinner applied behavior analysis to the institution of marriage.

Elsewhere in his writing he speaks at length about the ways in which cultures (families, friends, clergy people, neighbors, etc.) reinforce practices which tend to insure the survival of the culture. Marriage would seem to be one of these since a form of cultural chaos would likely develop if there were no stable marriages.

Meaning

To say that... behaviors have different "meanings" is only another way of saying that they are controlled by different variables.[20] *(p. 257)*

Author Note:

Some have said that Skinner rendered behavior meaningless by explaining it. On the contrary, Skinner felt that he had given it more meaning. Any particular activity has its greatest meaning to a person when he or she understands the variables that cause it.

Memories

The Inner Man is often said to store and recall memories. His behavior in doing so is much like that of the Outer Man when he makes records and puts them aside to be used at a later date...But how can the Inner Man do it? With what organs can he receive stimuli and make copies of them? Of what stuff are the copies made? In what space does he store them? How does he label them so that he can find them again? How does he scan the labels in the storehouse of memory to find a particular copy?...

We shall not put Cognitive Man in good order by discovering the space in which he works, for it is the work which is the bad metaphor. A man need not copy the stimulating environment in order to perceive it, and he need not make a copy in order to perceive it in the future. When an organism exposed to a set of contingencies of reinforcement is modified by them and as a result behaves in a different way in the future, we do not need to say that it stores the contingencies. What is "stored" is a modified organism, not a record of the modifying variables.[18] (p. 25,60)

Author Note:

Cognitive psychologists theorize that memories are stored for later recall and use. Skinner allowed that this is a relatively good description of what happens, for lay persons. However, such use of lay persons' terms by behavioral scientists was unacceptable to him.

For example, to say that a person is able to read French because he has stored memories of how to do it (and he recalls those memories as needed) explains nothing, according to Skinner. The reason it explains nothing is because it tells nothing about the hundreds of hours of study that likely went into study of French, nothing about the role models the person may have listened to who also read French, nothing of the instructions from a French teacher, or any other learning experiences that the person underwent.

Skinner also objected to the cognitive metaphor of storage and recall of memories because it was just that--a metaphor. People are not file cabinets, their brains are not computers (although that may be a convenient analogy). A science of behavior will be detoured rather than well served by elevating such metaphors to the status of events that are presumed to actually take place.

Mentalism

In the traditional mentalistic view,...a person is a member of the human species who behaves as he does because of many internal characteristics or possessions, among them sensations, habits, intelligence, opinions, dreams, personalities, moods, decisions, fantasies, skills, percepts, thoughts, virtues, intentions, abilities, instincts, daydreams, incentives, acts of will, joy, compassion, perceptual defenses, beliefs, responsibilities, elation, memories, needs, wisdom, wants, a death instinct, a sense of duty, sublimation, impulses, capacities, purposes, wishes, an id, repressed fears, a sense of shame, extraversion, images, knowledge, interests, information, a superego, propositions, experiences, attitudes, conflicts, meanings, reaction formations, a will to live, consciousness, anxiety, depression, fear, reason, libido, psychic energy, reminiscences, inhibitions, and mental illnesses.[5] (p.228-9)

Author Note:

Elsewhere Skinner wrote that it is perfectly natural to discover the workings of a watch by looking inside it. However the same is not true for humans. Yet, throughout history we have invented innumerable terms to describe events presumed to be happening inside people which perfectly "explain" an activity that we have observed.

Skinner called these pseudo explanations "mentalisms." Some of them, he felt, are fiction and do not exist (id, super ego, ego, instinct, etc.) while he believed others exist but do not cause behavior (anxiety, depression, etc.).

In his later years Skinner sometimes said that if he accomplished anything in his lifelong devotion to behavioral science he hoped it would be to have stamped out mentalistic "explanations" of behavior.

Mind

The exploration of the emotional and motivational life of the mind has been described as one of the great achievements in the history of human thought, but it is possible that it has been one of the great disasters. In its search for internal explanation, supported by the false sense of cause associated with feelings and introspective observations, mentalism has obscured the environmental antecedents which would have led to a much more effective analysis...

The argonauts of the psyche have for centuries sailed the stormy seas of the mind, never in sight of their goal, revising their charts from time to time in the light of what seemed like new information, less and less sure of their way home, hopelessly lost. They have failed to find the Golden Fleece.[5] (p. 182-3)

Author Note:

This quotation by Skinner says much about his point of view. Clearly, Skinner viewed the "mind" as another form of mentalism (see "Mentalism") - one that has cost us dearly. It has directed us away from the causes of our behavior (our genes and environments) and taken us down the seductive path of inner causation.

The second sentence in the first paragraph makes an important point. Because we typically have internal behaviors (feelings, for example) at the same time as, or slightly preceding, overt behaviors, we often mistakenly credit those feelings as the causes of our overt activity. We may say that we are going to the concert because we feel excited. This is wrong and would be better stated as follows: We are going to the concert *and* we feel excited because previous concerts have been enjoyable and exciting (reinforcing).

In the second paragraph, Skinner compares traditional psychologists, who persist in looking for the causes of behavior inside us (in minds, cognitions, unconscious conflicts, etc.) to mythical argonauts, searching for a nonexistent golden fleece, hopelessly lost, drifting further from home.

Money

A generalized reinforcer distinguished by its physical specifications is the token. The commonest example is money. It is the generalized reinforcer par excellence because, although "money won't buy everything," it can be exchanged for primary reinforcers of great variety.[2] (p. 79)

Author Note:

Our system of money is a large scale token economy. It is efficient, it is highly useful, and its existence goes generally unquestioned in a capitalist democracy.

It also is a system of secondary reinforcers. These are reinforcers that of themselves have little or no intrinsic value but can be exchanged for things that do have intrinsic value, called primary reinforcers.

The individual who believes that "reinforcement would not work" for him need only be asked whether money is at all rewarding to him.

W. Joseph Wyatt

N

Needs

Man is not "in bondage" to his needs; he is not "driven by greed or lust." If such statements can be paraphrased at all, he is in bondage to the things which gratify his needs... The greedy or lustful man is... suffering from a particularly effective schedule of reinforcement.[1] (p. 65-66)

Author Note:

One more mentalism (see "Mentalism") that is erroneously used to explain behavior is the "need." If we do not know why a person did a thing we may give the appearance of explaining it by saying that he did it because he had a "need" to do it. We may say that a baby cries because it has a need to cry, or that a gambler persists at losing money because he has a need to gamble. These explain nothing and simply lead us further from discovering the true causes of the behaviors, causes which lie in the environmental and genetic histories of the person.

Nervousness

When effective escape is impossible... a highly aversive condition may evoke ineffective behavior in the form of aimless wandering or searching. Simple "nervousness" is often of this sort.[2] (p. 364)

Author Note:

Skinner believed that anxiety is most often the result of punishment, especially punishment from which there is little or no escape or which may have been particularly severe and may loom as possible again.

Nervous System

Eventually a science of the nervous system based upon direct observation rather than inference will describe the neural states and events which immediately precede instances of behavior. We shall know the precise neurological conditions which immediately precede, say, the response, "No thank you." These events in turn will be found to be preceded by other neurological events, and these in turn by others. This series will lead us back to events outside the nervous system and, eventually, outside the organism.[2] (p. 28)

Author Note:

Elsewhere we have seen that Skinner had interest in what happens inside a person (see, for example, "Thinking" and "Feeling"). This quotation makes it clear that he is humbled by the enormous task faced by physiological psychologists and others who undertake the study of what occurs biologically inside an organism when it behaves.

Ultimately, though, a functional analysis will always be necessary in order to have a complete science of behavior, no matter how complete our understanding of the inside biological story may be.

W. Joseph Wyatt

Novelists

It is significant that the novelist, as a specialist in the description of human behavior, often shows an early history in which social reinforcement has been especially important.[3] (p. 303)

Author Note:

It is a verbal community which allows us to describe our behavior, both external and internal behavior.

Those who are particularly adept at describing behavior, such as novelists, have often been reinforced for producing such verbal descriptions from an early age.

What is not stated here is that Skinner himself wrote one novel and began his career hoping to be a novelist. He spent a self-described dark year in which he failed rather badly at that task. He never lost his admiration for those who became successful novelists.

O

Operant

A response which has already occurred cannot, of course, be predicted or controlled. We can only predict that similar responses will occur in the future. The unit of a predictive science is, therefore, not a response but a class of responses. The word "operant" will be used to describe this class. The term emphasizes the fact that the behavior operates upon the environment to generate consequences. The consequences define the properties with respect to which responses are called similar. The term will be used both as an adjective (operant behavior) and as a noun to designate the behavior defined by a given consequence.[2] *(p. 64-5)*

Author Note:

To those who have read very little of Skinner this quotation is likely rather murky. But it need not be highly confusing. The key sentence is the fifth one which contains the word "operate."

From the word operate Skinner devised the term "operant." An operant is a type, or a class, of behavior, which gets a certain result (consequence).

For example, in a laboratory "Skinner box" rats were trained to press a bar in order to get a bite of food. A given rat may have pressed the bar with its right paw on one occasion, its left paw on another occasion, its nose on another occasion, or its flank on a fourth occasion. Bar pressing is the operant, the class of behavior which generates the consequence (the bite of food).

At a complex human level consider the operant class known as gambling. A person might engage in it by pulling on a one-armed bandit, rolling dice, playing cards, or any one of a number of other ways. The occasional win is the consequence which defines the class of behavior (the operant) known as gambling.

Thus, an operant is a class of behavior (bar pressing, gambling) which is defined by its consequences (a bite of food, an occasional win) for the organism (rat, person). Note that the consequences need not happen every time that the operant behavior occurs. Just as the operant known as gambling may be maintained by a rare win, the operant known as bar pressing (in rats) may be maintained by only one bite of food for every hundred or more bar presses.

Originality

Man is now in much better control of the world than were his ancestors, and this suggests a progress in discovery and invention in which there appears to be a strong element of originality. But we could express this fact just as well by saying that the environment is now in better control of man. Reinforcing contingencies shaped the behavior of the individual, and novel contingencies generate novel forms of behavior.[2] *(p. 255)*

Author Note:

The temperature drops and a person turns up the heat. An outbreak of flu is predicted with the result that an individual takes a preventive flu shot. Hearing a report of rain a person grabs the umbrella before leaving the house. But have humans developed these clever ways to overcome the rigors of their environments because they possess a trait of originality?

Not really, according to Skinner. For it is the environment which exerts control over the person, leading the person gradually, often by trial and error, to develop novel methods of exerting countercontrol over the environment.

P

Pavlov

I bought Pavlov's book and took it with me to Greenwich Village, where I spent several Bohemian months before going on to Harvard. I read Pavlov by day and sowed wild oats by night. I am sure Pavlov himself would have approved of this pairing of stimuli. Even today a page of his book elicits many warm, if somewhat faded, autonomic responses.[21] *(p. 74)*

Author Note:

In the 1920s Skinner "sowed wild oats" in Greenwich Village, New York, for a summer before beginning his graduate study at Harvard. During that time he was influenced by his reading of Pavlov's classical conditioning work. These were the experiments with classically conditioned dog salivation, known to all introductory psychology students.

This quotation gives us a glimpse of Skinner's humor. In the same way that Pavlov's dogs salivated on hearing a conditioned response (a bell), Skinner admits having developed a classically conditioned response (sexual arousal) that occurs on reading a page of Pavlov's book (the conditioned stimulus which causes that sexual arousal).

Permissiveness

Permissiveness is not,... a policy; it is the abandonment of policy, and its apparent advantages are illusory. To refuse to control is to leave control not to the person himself, but to other parts of the social and nonsocial environments.[3] (p. 79)

Author Note:

To be permissive, such as with children, leaves them vulnerable to accidental influences which may be quite bad for them. To say that the child will decide what is best for it is to say that parental control has been abandoned. Whatever accidental sources of control exist in the environment are then the factors that influence the child to do what it does.

Personality

Is the scientific study of behavior--whether normal or psychotic--concerned with the behavior of the observable organism under the control of hereditary and environmental factors, or with the functioning of one or more personalities engaged in a variety of mental processes under the prompting of instincts, needs, emotions, memories, and habits? I do not want to raise the question of the supposed nature of these inner entities. A certain kinship between such an explanatory system and primitive animism can scarcely be missed...[4] (p. 264)

Author Note:

"Personality" represents another example of the kind of explanatory fiction which Skinner stood against. While he had no objection to describing an individual as friendly, angry, or non-assertive, he objected greatly to attaching the word personality to these descriptive terms and giving the illusion of explaining the behavior of the person. We explain nothing by saying that behavior is the result of a friendly personality, an angry personality, or a non-assertive personality presumed to exist inside the individual.

For Skinner these were good descriptions but poor explanations. In fact, they explained behavior no better than primitive animistic explanations involving spirits and the like. The real explanations lie in our genetic and environmental histories.

Physiologist

The physiologist of the future will tell us all that can be known about what is happening inside the behaving organism... He will be able to show how an organism is changed when exposed to contingencies of reinforcement and why the changed organism then behaves in a different way, possibly at a much later date. What he discovers cannot invalidate the laws of a science of behavior, but it will make the picture of human action more nearly complete.[5] (p. 236-7)

Author Note:

What happens inside people when they run, feel fear, breathe, communicate? The inside story was of importance to Skinner. He believed that it would ultimately be disclosed by the physiologist.

In contrast, traditional psychologists have postulated any number of things (conflicts, needs, drives, etc.) that might be going on inside people. These have little or no explanatory power, in Skinner's view. But discovery of the physiological activities that take place inside an organism does not mean that we will know the causes of its observable behavior. Rather, the inside activities are simply more behaviors which are themselves in need of explanation. And for that we always must look to the outside influences.

Private Events (1)

Other common objects of introspection are proprio-ceptive and interoceptive stimuli and (particularly important in the case of feelings) responses of the autonomic nervous system. It would be absurd to deny the existence of events of this kind or the possibility that a person may respond to them and learn to describe them. It is equally absurd to argue that because they occur inside the skin they have non-physical dimensions.[1] (p. 242)

Author Note:

Skinner referred to activities taking place inside the skin as "private events." He is often wrongly accused of believing that nothing important takes place inside us. Also erroneous is the assertion by those who insist that Skinner took the position that people have no thoughts or feelings.

For Skinner it would be equally wrong to say, "I hugged him because I love him," as to say, "I love him because I hugged him." The feeling of love and the hug occur at roughly the same time but one does not cause the other. Other variables cause both the hug and the feeling that accompanies it.

Private Events (2)

The distinction between public and private is by no means the same as that between physical and mental. That is why methodological behaviorism (which adopts the first) is very different from radical behaviorism (which lops off the latter term in the second). The result is that while the radical behaviorist may in some cases consider private events (inferentially, perhaps, but none the less meaningfully), the methodological operationist has maneuvered himself into a position where he cannot.[22] (p. 277)

Author Note:

Skinner drew a distinction between his brand of behaviorism, which he called radical (meaning thoroughgoing) behaviorism, and earlier versions such as that practiced by John B. Watson, called methodological behaviorism.

Watson had excluded private events (thoughts and feelings) from study because they were not publicly observable. However, Skinner believed that the behaviors happening inside our bodies are fair game for study, provided we conceptualize them as occurring in the realm of matter and energy with which the natural sciences deal.

It is not internal behaviors to which Skinner objected. Rather, he objected to unscientific conceptualizations of inner behaviors.

Psychoanalysis

Psychoanalysis has come closest to supplying a common formulation (of man), but it arose as a form of therapy and some touch of psychopathology survives when it is applied to everyday life. In spite of many claims to the contrary, it has not contributed a workable theory which is generally useful.[1] (p. 97)

Author Note:

Despite the friction between behavior analysts and psychoanalysts Skinner was able to appreciate the fact that the psychoanalysts had worked hard to develop a theory which attempted to explain all of human behavior. Psychoanalytic theory, although rich and expansive, has contributed little that is valid or useful, according to Skinner.

Psychotherapy (1)

The field of psychotherapy is rich in explanatory fictions. Behavior itself has not been accepted as a subject matter in its own right, but only as an indication of something wrong somewhere else. The task of therapy is said to be to remedy an inner illness of which the behavioral manifestations are merely "symptoms"... We have seen enough of inner causes to understand why this doctrine has given psychotherapy an impossible assignment. It is not an inner cause of behavior but the behavior itself which--in the medical analogy of catharsis--must be "got out of the system."[2] (p. 272-3)

Author Note:

In traditional psychotherapy, particularly psychoanalytic psychotherapy, maladaptive feelings, thoughts and activities are viewed as symptoms of underlying psychological conflicts. The observed problem behavior is not the focus of treatment. Rather, the hypothesized underlying conflict becomes the focus of treatment.

For example, the bed-wetting child may be thought of as suffering an unconscious conflict which is manifested at a surface level by the bed-wetting. Treatment focuses on the underlying symptom with little attention to the bed-wetting itself, in the traditional view.

Skinner took an alternative approach--that the bed-wetting is the problem and should be treated directly.

Skinner's approach led traditional psychotherapists to predict that "symptom substitution," would result. This meant that the symptom (bed-wetting) might seemingly be alleviated by behavioral treatment only to be replaced by a new symptom (perhaps declining grades in school) that would emerge because the underlying conflict had not been treated. Skinner and the other behavior analysts rejected that proposition.

Several decades of intense and broad ranging behavioral research have validated Skinner's point of view.

Psychotherapy (2)

Psychotherapy has been much more explicitly committed to mentalistic systems than has education. The illness which is the object of therapy is called mental, and we have already examined Freud's mental apparatus and a few intrapsychic processes said to be disturbed or deranged in the mentally ill. What is wrong is usually explored in the realm of feelings.[5] (p. 204)

Author Note:

As with many other of Skinner's quotations, here is another statement of his view that it is a mistake to think of internal processes as somehow outside the realm of the natural sciences, a mistake to view them as if they were comprised of something other than the matter and energy with which natural sciences deal.

But here Skinner goes a step further and makes the connection between that sort of mentalism and feelings. Specifically, because feelings occur inside of us and usually occur simultaneously with observable behavior, they have often been wrongly assumed to be made of some nonphysical (mental) stuff or material.

Punishment (1)

Extinction is an effective way of removing an operant from the repertoire of an organism. It should not be confused with other procedures designed to have the same effect. The currently preferred technique is punishment, which...involves different processes and is of questionable effectiveness.[2] (p. 71)

Author Note:

Skinner recognized that there are many ways to control behavior. It is, perhaps, rather odd that he is often wrongly viewed as advocating punitive methods of control, when in fact he is also quite widely known because he advocated positive reinforcement.

Here he articulates an alternative to punishment that does not involve positive reinforcement. It is "extinction." It means the disappearance of a behavior because it has not been reinforced, because it no longer "works" for the person, because it no longer gets the person what he or she wants.

A good example is the advice of the telephone company where harassing phone calls are concerned. Hang up. This takes away the reinforcing value of the call for the caller. Without that reinforcement the caller will ultimately quit calling.

Punishment (2)

The trouble is that when we punish a person for behaving badly, we leave it up to him to discover how to behave well.[3] (p. 62)

Author Note:

Skinner is describing another problem in the use of punishment, another reason why he felt it best to use positive reinforcement to get an individual to do what we would like for him to do. Specifically, when we punish a person for doing a thing we have only taught him what *not* to do. We have failed to teach him any better activity he might do instead.

Punishment *(3)*

Nature if not God has created man in such a way that he can be controlled punitively. People quickly become skillful punishers (if not, thereby, skillful controllers), whereas alternative positive measures are not easily learned. The need for punishment seems to have the support of history, and alternative practices threaten the cherished values of freedom and dignity. And we go on punishing-and defending punishment.[3] (p. 75)

Author Note:

If punishment is so bad why do most people persist in using it? The answer is that it works quickly to suppress an unwanted behavior. It takes more time and effort to use positive methods to eliminate the same behavior or replace it with an improved behavior.

For example, a teacher may punish a student's talking out by taking away break time. The problem with this is that it fails to teach the student how to get attention in more positive ways (assuming that talking out was maintained by the attention that it had been receiving).

A second facet of this quotation is Skinner's interest in the uses of punishment to defend our "cherished values of freedom and dignity." Our judicial-legal system is based upon the assumption that people are free to do right or wrong and that those who do the wrong things deserve to be punished.   And certainly there are many instances in which incarceration or other forms of punishment are needed in order to protect society from the dangerous person.

Skinner noticed that when we begin to think in positive terms rather than punitive terms with regard to the control of human behavior, a frequent concern is raised that we would be unable to hold people responsible for their crimes, unable to punish them, if we wholeheartedly adopted his philosophy.

Purpose (1)

Possibly no charge is more often leveled against behaviorism or a science of behavior than that it cannot deal with purpose or intention. A stimulus-response formula has no answer, but operant behavior is the very field of purpose and intention. By its nature it is directed toward the future: a person acts in order that something will happen, and the order is temporal.[5] (p. 61)

Author Note:

Among the misrepresentations of Skinner's philosophy is that he leaves us no "purpose in life." But Skinner carefully defined purpose in terms of operant conditioning. In layman's terms the worker, to use an employment example, works because his purpose is to get money, job satisfaction or some other reward. More simply stated, and preferred by Skinner, is that the reinforcer, money, maintains the behavior, work.

Purpose (2)

An important role of autonomous man has been to give human   behavior direction, and it is often said that in dispossessing an inner agent we leave man himself without a purpose...The primate hand evolved in order that things might be more successfully manipulated, but its purpose is to be found not in a prior design but rather in the process of selection. Similarly, in operant conditioning the purpose of skilled movement of the hand is to be found in the consequences which follow it. A pianist neither acquires nor executes the behavior of playing a scale smoothly because of a prior intention of doing so. Smoothly played scales are reinforcing for many reasons, and they select skilled movements. In neither the evolution of the human hand nor in the acquired use of the hand is any prior intention or purpose at issue.[3] (p. 194-5)

Author Note:

In reformulating the concepts of purpose and intention Skinner became the target of much criticism. But he persisted throughout his career in attempting to make one thing clear--we explain nothing when we say that an individual did a thing because it was his "purpose" to do it or because he "intended" to do it. That tells you only that he did it, not why he did it.

To understand why it was done we generally have to look at the reinforcers for it. To say that a pianist played a scale smoothly because, "it was his purpose," or because, "he intended to," fails to acknowledge the hours of practice, the feedback from teachers and other listeners, the sounds of the scales themselves feeding back to the pianist. Those are the reasons that a pianist plays a scale smoothly. Those kinds of reasons are the "why" of all behavior.

Purpose (3)

...When a person is "aware of his purpose," he is feeling or observing introspectively a condition produced by reinforcement.[5] *(p. 63)*

Author Note:

Often we feel we have a "sense of purpose" when we are about to do a thing, particularly a noteworthy thing. What that amounts to, in Skinner's view, is that we recognize certain internal bodily sensations as being similar to sensations we have felt on previous occasions when we did something special. This does not negate or deny the sense of purpose. It merely puts it in its place and in perspective.

Q

Quantity of Behavior

Sheer quantity of behavior is important. Other things being equal a culture will be more likely to uncover an original artist if it induces many people to paint pictures, or to turn up a great composer if it induces many people to compose... Sheer quantity of behavior is also important in the individual. The great Mozart symphonies are a selection from a large number; the great Picassos are only part of the product of a lifetime of painting. [23] *(p. 182)*

Author Note:

Everything else being equal, the more activity that a person produces, the more likely some of it will be reinforced. The more paintings attempted, the more likely someone will respond favorably to at least one of them. Naturally there are limits to this axiom. It is possible that quality may be subserviated to quantity to an extent that the individual suffers a net loss in rewards.

Quotation

It is easy to fall back upon quotations in lieu of composition, but also easy to use the nearest available quotation although it is inaccurate. Quotation, as Bertrand Russell said of hypotheses, has the advantage of thievery over honest toil. [24] *(p. 297)*

Author Note:

People quote other people because it is easy. Or at least it is easier than composing one's own quotations, in many instances. This book is no exception.

R

Reinforcement

Events which are found to be reinforcing are of two sorts. Some reinforcements consist of presenting stimuli, of adding something--for example, food, water or sexual contact--to the situation. These we call positive reinforcers. Others consist of removing something--for example, a loud noise, a very bright light, extreme cold or heat, or electric shock--from the situation.   These we call negative reinforcers. In both cases the effect of reinforcement is the same--the probability of response is increased.[2] (p. 73)

Author Note:

Reinforcement is what people always want. But, more accurately, it is not people who are reinforced. Rather, it is their behavior.

And reinforcement is defined functionally.   A reinforcer is any stimulus that results in the increased probability of the behavior which preceded it.

And reinforcement is of two types.   Positive reinforcers are those things such as food, water, and sexual contact that we want. Negative reinforcers are those things that we want to get away from. For example, getting away from the extreme heat of an unairconditioned office on a muggy August after-noon is negatively reinforcing. It gets rid of something unpleasant.

But both positive and negative reinforcement have

W. Joseph Wyatt

the same net result. They increase the probability that we will act similarly when in the same or similar circumstances.

Religion

A religious agency is a special form of government under which "good" and "bad" become "pious" and "sinful." Contingencies involving positive and negative reinforcement, often of the most extreme sort, are codified--for example, as commandments--and maintained by specialists, usually with the support of ceremonies, rituals, and stories.[3] (p. 110)

Author Note:

A behavior analytic view of traditional religion has brought about criticism of behavior analysis, and Skinner, by organized religion.

Here Skinner is drawing a comparison between government and religion (which historically were one and the same). Both have their laws and the laws involve both positive and negative reinforcers, as well as punishers (incarceration, fines, etc. in the case of government; consignment to Hell in the case of religion).

Responsibility

The real issue is the effectiveness of techniques of control. We shall not solve the problems of alcoholism and juvenile delinquency by increasing a sense of responsibility. It is the environment which is "responsible" for the objectional behavior, and it is the environment, not some at-

tribute of the individual, which must be changed. [3] *(p. 70)*

Author Note:

We sometimes hear it said that a person's problems will be solved if only he will take responsibility for them. To Skinner this was an illusory prescription because we still are left wondering how to get an individual to take responsibility. To do that we always will look to the environment, to the sources of potential control over the individual.

As an example, consider the case of the alcoholic who is much more likely to "take responsibility" for his alcoholism if he is threatened with losing his job, his family, or other things that are important to him. These environmental influences exert control and often have the effect of changing his behavior. Skinner felt that we gain nothing by leaping to the conclusion that these factors create a "sense of responsibility" which then does the real work of curbing excessive drinking.

S

Science (1)

The methods of science have been enormously successful wherever they have been tried. Let us then apply them to human affairs.[2] *(p. 5)*

Author Note:

It is likely that there is no other single quotation which more clearly and concisely expresses Skinner's outlook toward, and frustration with, behavioral science as it has come to be known and practiced by the majority of psychologists.

Curiously, we praise the methods and outcomes of science in every field except the field of human behavior. Mentalistic explanations of behavior such as those hypothesized by Freud (id, ego, super ego, etc.) are, to Skinner, fictions not based on scientific findings. Likewise, the explanatory forces (actualization potential, growth drive) alleged by the humanistic phenomenologists, while more pleasant sounding and uplifting, are no more scientific than Freud's mental apparatus.

Although this quotation is from 1953, Skinner marveled until his death at the evidently limitless capacity of psychologists to engage in everything except what he considered to be actual behavioral science. Just prior to his death he pointed out his strong belief that the most recent "fad," cognitive science, was but another wayward effort to explain behavior by appealing to inner mental events (short and long-term memory), which explained nothing.

This is not to say that Skinner rejected the notion that people have memories of recent and remote events. Rather, he rejected the notion that these explain the "why" of behavior.

Science (2)

There is one difficulty, however. The application of science to human behavior is not so simple as it seems. Most of those who advocate it are simply looking for "the facts." To them science is little more than careful observation...But the way in which science has been applied in other fields shows that something more is involved. Science is not concerned just with "getting the facts," after which one may act with greater wisdom in an unscientific fashion. Science supplies its own wisdom...

Science is more than the mere description of events as they occur. It is an attempt to discover order, to show that certain events stand in lawful relations to other events. No practical technology can be based upon science until such relations have been discovered. But order is not only a possible end product; it is a working assumption which must be adopted at the very start...If we are to use the methods of science in the field of human affairs, we must assume that behavior is lawful and determined.[2] (p. 6)

Author Note:

It is reasonable to assume that behavior is either lawful or it is random and capricious. Either there is a cause for everything, or behavior is random and we will never discover its causes.

Skinner's fundamental assumption was that behavior is lawful. He believed that a science of behavior must operate under that assumption. Thus, in addition to conducting scientific investigations, he was interested in the philosophy of science and the assumptions that underlie scientific inquiry.

Scientific Behavior (1)

Scientific behavior is possibly the most complex subject matter ever submitted to scientific analysis, and we are still far from having an adequate account of it...a functional analysis which not only clarifies the nature of scientific inquiry but suggests how it may be most effectively imparted to young scientists still lies in the future. [1] *(p. X-XI)*

Author Note:

The behavior of scientists ought to be studied. Scandals in academia and other research settings in which it has been shown that scientists "fudge" data, provide us with reason to agree.

However, for Skinner there was another reason as well. That is, in order to produce more science we must understand how it is that scientific behavior is developed in a person. To give Skinner credit, he was, in this quotation, suggesting that his and all scientists' behavior be functionally analyzed to determine the influences on it.

Scientific Behavior (2)

It is perhaps natural that psychologists should awaken

only slowly to the possibility that behavioral processes may be directly observed, or that they should only gradually put the older statistical and theoretical techniques in their proper perspective. But it is time to insist that science does not progress by carefully designed steps called "experiments" each of which has a well-defined beginning and end. Science is a continuous and often a disorderly and accidental process.[25] *(p. 231)*

Author Note:

This appeared in the flagship journal of the American Psychological Association in 1956. Skinner had become quite disenchanted with what he perceived to be the lock step style into which mainstream psychology had fallen.

Elsewhere Skinner once wrote that when a behavioral scientist finds something interesting he should drop everything else and study it. This openness to new data, new ideas, and new experimentation has been lost on mainstream psychology, in Skinner's view.

The Self

We may quarrel with any analysis which appeals to a self or personality as an inner determiner of action, but the facts which have been represented with such devices cannot be ignored.[2] *(p. 284)*

Author Note:

If traditional explanations of behavior based on the action of an inner agent or being (a "self" or a "personality") were wrong, Skinner was careful to make it clear that there was at least some legitimacy involved in such an analysis.

Specifically, the behaviors wrongly attributed to these fictional inner agents always need to be understood. We should not ignore them, and Skinner did not wish to be thought of as ignoring them simply because he did not accept mentalistic "explanations" of them.

Self-Control

The notion of personal credit is incompatible with the hypothesis that human behavior is wholly determined by genetic and environmental forces. The hypothesis is sometimes said to imply that man is a helpless victim, but we must not overlook the extent to which he controls the things which control him. Man is largely responsible for the environment in which he lives. He has changed the physical world to minimize aversive properties and maximize positive reinforcements, and he has constructed governmental, religious, educational, economic, and psychotherapeutic systems which promote satisfying personal contacts and make him more skillful, informed, productive, and happy. He is engaged in a gigantic exercise in self-control. [26]

Author Note:

Skinner rejected free will and self-control as explanations of behavior. These were to Skinner nothing more than fictions which obscured the real causes of our behavior, causes which lie in the environmental and genetic influences upon us.

However, at another level Skinner recognized that

people do exert a type of self-control. This is because they are able to respond to elements of their environments. For example, institutions such as government, religion, education, etc. have been devised by people as ways of controlling or minimizing some of the negative features of our world (and maximizing some of the positives). Thus, it is more accurate to say that Skinner viewed us as engaging in mutual control between person and environment, rather than in self-control.

Single Subject Experimentation

Another accident rescued me from mechanized statistics and brought me back to an even more intensive concentration on the single case. In essence, I suddenly found myself face to face with the engineering problem of the animal trainer. When you have the responsibility of making absolutely sure that a given organism will engage in a given sort of behavior at a given time, you quickly grow impatient with theories of learning.

Principles, hypotheses, theorems, satisfactory proof at the .05 level of significance that behavior at a choice point shows the effect of secondary reinforcement--nothing could be more irrelevant. No one goes to the circus to see the average dog jump through a hoop significantly oftener than untrained dogs raised under the same circumstances, or to see an elephant demonstrate a principle of behavior.[25] *(p. 227)*

Author Note:

Psychological research typically involves comparisons between groups of individuals to determine whether groups receiving different treatments will cause them to act differently. Often the results show that, on average, the groups differ significantly. But the average for each group is only a rough approximation to the activity and behavior of any individual in that group.

Skinner believed that the activities of the individual were being overlooked, subserviated to the group averages, in standard psychological research. In this quotation he is arguing forcefully for attention to individual experimental subjects.

Skinner is often accused by his critics, many of whom are traditional psychologists devoted to "average" findings, of stripping away the importance of the individual (by insisting that people are not motivated by internal forces, needs, drives, will, etc.). But when it comes to knowing what an individual will do and being able to accurately predict it, Skinner insisted that nothing could be more important.

Smoking

The distinction between need and reinforcement is clarified by a current problem. Many of those who are trying to stop smoking cigarettes will testify to a basic drive or need as powerful as those of hunger, sex, and aggression. (For those who have a genuine drug addiction, smoking is reinforced in part by the alleviation of withdrawal symptoms, but most smokers can shift to nicotine-free cigarettes without too much trouble. They are still unable to control the powerful repertoire of responses which compose smoking.) It is clear that the troublesome pattern of behavior--"the cigarette habit"--can be traced, not to a need, but to a history of reinforcement because there was no problem before the discovery of tobacco or before the invention of the cigarette as an especially reinforcing form in which tobacco may be smoked.

Whatever their other needs may have been, our ancestors had no need to smoke cigarettes, and no one has the need today if, like them, he has never been reinforced for smoking.[19] (p. 162)

Author Note:

It is interesting that in the richness of Skinner's writings there are many examples of his attention to everyday activities of humans. In this analysis of cigarette smoking Skinner takes pains to point out that we explain nothing by saying that we engage in a behavior because we "need" to do it or because we "have a need" to do it.

Cigarette smokers know about the "powerful repertoire of responses" of which Skinner wrote. The behaviors in this repertoire are like links in a chain. The behaviors link up until the final link, smoking the cigarette, is achieved. While the removal of withdrawal symptoms that comes with smoking explains the continuation of the habit, it does not explain the start of it. Nor does it explain why someone who has once quit smoking would return to it weeks or months later. The explanation? The entire chain does not disappear simply because its final link has (at least temporarily) been removed.

W. Joseph Wyatt

Statistics (1)

The experimental control or elimination of a variable is the heart of a laboratory science, and, in general, it is to be preferred to manipulation through statistical treatment.[27] *(p. 22)*

Author Note:
As with several other quotations contained herein, this is another instance in which Skinner has taken to task some of the traditional experimental methods in psychology. In particular, Skinner much preferred working with an individual subject to see what it would do under various laboratory conditions than with a large group of subjects (or many groups) whose average behavior was found and compared to the average behavior of some other large group.

Statistics (2)

How simple it is to match groups of subjects, devise a crude measure of the behavior at issue, arrange for tests to be administered, and punch the IBM cards! No matter what comes of it all, no one can say that work has not been done. Statistics will even see to it that the result will be "significant" even if it is proved to mean nothing.[28] *(p. 320)*

Author Note:
As with the immediately preceding quotation Skinner again takes issue with traditional behavioral science in which average functioning of large groups of subjects is compared. If there are many subjects per group then even modest differences in the group

averages take on "statistical significance." Yet the differences in the group averages may be relatively meaningless in the real world. They may give us virtually no insight into the activities of any individual member of any group.

Superstition

Rituals for changing one's luck at cards are good examples (of superstition). A few accidental connections between a ritual and favorable consequences suffice to set up and maintain the behavior in spite of many unreinforced instances. The bowler who has released a ball down the alley but continues to behave as if he were controlling it by twisting and turning his arm and shoulder is another case in point.[29] *(p. 170)*

Author Note:

Superstitious activity is usually the result of accidental reinforcement or accidental punishment. "Step on a crack, break your mother's back," probably originated in an instance where a person was searching for the explanation of his mother's broken back. Lacking a better explanation, in a primitive culture he may have attributed it to the most recent thing he had done.

The same is probably true for other superstitions such as those in athletics. A player who performs well may not change his shirt or socks, particularly if he can see no other reason for his especially good performance that day. It is the accidental connection between what a person does and some good or bad fortune, usually immediately following, that maintains a superstition.

Survival of Cultures

We produce cultural "mutations" when we invent new social practices, and we change the conditions under which they are selected when we change the environments in which men live.

To refuse to do either of these things is to leave further changes in our culture to accident, and accident is the tyrant really to be feared.[26]

Author Note:

That it would be totalitarian is a misrepresentation of Skinner's vision of Utopia. He believed that cultures are always controlled and that the people in them are always controlled. The goal is simply a matter of selecting the best form of control, the one which would ensure the survival of a culture.

This is different from totalitarianism and, actually, would serve to protect us from totalitarianism, which Skinner saw as a possible result when members of a culture do not acknowledge that they are always controlled. Failure to acknowledge the possibility of control increases the likelihood that we may potentially be controlled by a tyrant.

T

Teaching Machines

In the light of what we know about differential contingencies of reinforcement, the world of the young child is shamefully impoverished. And only machines will remedy this, for the required frequency and subtlety of reinforcement cannot otherwise be arranged.[11] *(p. 361)*

Author Note:

> Skinner strongly favored the use of teaching machines to enhance learning. It is unfortunate that he has been opposed by many, especially educators, for his advocacy of teaching machines. Ironically, education is now flooded with demands by educators, parents and legislators that students be exposed to and taught by computers.

Theory

Behavior can only be satisfactorily understood by going beyond the facts themselves. What is needed is a theory of behavior, but the term theory is in such bad repute that I hasten to explain. Psychology has had no worse theories than any other science, but it has had them more recently, and they have suffered in the light of our improved understanding of scientific method...

Facts and theories do not stand in opposition to each other. The relation, rather, is this: theories are based upon facts; they are statements about organizations of facts...

...the two great explanatory systems which have held

the psychological field for a hundred years are no longer paying their way...

One of these explanatory theories is the notion of a controlling mind. From our modern vantage point the essentially fictional nature of this explanation is clear. It is on a par with the abhorred vacuum or the vis viva *of phlogiston. Most of us like to feel that the ghost has been laid, and that we are free of mentalistic explanations. But the inner man, constructed of such stuff as dreams are made on, still flourishes. At least half the text books in psychology still talk about mental life...*

The other current explanatory theory flourishes with greater prestige and presumably in more robust health. This is the physiological theory of behavior. The inner man is given neurological properties, with a great gain in scientific respectability. Psychiatry becomes neuro-psychiatry, and psychology the study of the nervous system. It is difficult to attack this theory without seeming to criticize the physiological psychologist, but no criticism is involved.[27] *(p. 37-39)*

Author Note:

This lengthy quotation summarizes Skinner's view of theory.

It should be clear that Skinner is not opposed to all theory. It is only certain kinds of theory to which he objected. The first of these is the mentalistic theory of Sigmund Freud. Skinner compared it to the ancient animistic explanations of behavior which we have cast aside.

The second theory to which he objected is one that

continues to flourish. This is the physiological theory of behavior which Skinner believed to be a mistaken exercise in non-explanation. We frequently hear talk from adherents to the physiological theory which would lead us to believe that the causes of our actions may best be understood by looking at the central nervous system. No doubt there are instances when this is true such as when an individual behaves bizarrely and is found to have a brain tumor, or to have been poisoned, or etc.

However, according to Skinner this does not excuse the recent tendency among some professionals to cavalierly attribute virtually all unusual behavior to central nervous system dysfunction or some other physical illness.

Thinking

Human thought is human behavior. The history of human thought is what people have said and done. Mathematical symbols are the products of written and spoken verbal behavior, and the concepts and relationships of which they are symbols are in the environment. Thinking has the dimensions of behavior, not of a fancied inner process which finds expression in behavior...

...The world of the mind is as remote today as it was when Plato is said to have discovered it. By attempting to move human behavior into a world of nonphysical dimensions, mentalistic or cognitive psychologists have cast the basic issues in insoluble forms. They have also probably cost us much useful evidence, because great thinkers (who presumably know what thinking is) have been led to report their activities in subjective terms, focusing on

their feelings and what they introspectively observe while thinking, and as a result they have failed to report significant facts about their earlier histories.[5] (p. 130-1)

Author Note:
Skinner conceptualized thinking as verbal behavior that could not be heard by anyone else, and as visual behavior (images or pictures in the mind's eye) that could not be seen by anyone else, etc.

But he was careful to point out that our thoughts are simply more behavior to be explained, and are not themselves explanations of other behavior. Thinking and visual imagery are learned and reinforced and subject to extinction and the other laws of behavior, like observable behavior.

And how do we explain thinking? Not by looking inward.   Rather we will explain it by looking outward and backward, to the reinforcement histories of people. Someone who is a critical thinker has probably had such thinking reinforced. Someone who is a pessimistic thinker has probably had such talk (and the thoughts accompanying it) reinforced with attention.   The individual who is a "free thinker" has probably met with approval or other rewards for demonstrating novel ideas to his friends or colleagues. In such reinforcement histories lie the roots of thinking.

U

The Unconscious

The behaviorist is often asked "What about the unconscious?" as if it presented an especially difficult problem, but the only problem is consciousness. All behavior is basically unconscious in the sense that it is shaped and maintained by contingencies which are effective even though they are not observed or otherwise analyzed. In some cultures, including our own, well-established practices of self-description generate consciousness in the present sense. We not only behave, we observe that we are behaving, and we observe the conditions under which we behave.[1] (p. 246)

Author Note:

For Skinner the unconscious mental apparatus of Freud and others was fictional. However, this did not mean that Skinner denied the existence of all types of unconscious processes.

Skinner did not believe in the physical existence of a portion of the mind that was "unconscious" and which contained forces (id, actualization potential, etc.) outside the realm of matter and energy with which a natural science deals. But he *did* allow for another sort of analysis of unconscious processes.

Specifically, he was well aware that we are often not able to articulate all of the variables (genetic and environmental) which cause us to do what we do. In that sense many of the causes of our behavior are "unconscious." But this is not to say that they are outside the realm of the natural sciences or that they are made of some mentalistic "stuff" which is not of the physical world.

Understanding

Understanding sometimes means knowing reasons. If I throw a switch to put a piece of apparatus into operation and nothing happens, I may try the switch again, but my behavior quickly undergoes extinction, and I may then look to see whether the apparatus is connected with the power source, or whether a fuse is blown, or whether the starting switch is broken. In doing so, I may come to understand why it has not worked. In the sense of discovering the reasons, I have acquired understanding by analyzing the prevailing contingencies.[5] (p. 156)

Author Note:

To say that I do an activity because I understand how to do it explains nothing, according to Skinner. Yet "understanding" is a term often used to explain what a person has done (As in, "He can do long division because he understands how to do it.").

At the same time there is a type of understanding which *is* worth analyzing--being able to articulate and act upon the causes of any phenomenon.

Unformalized Principle of Scientific Practice No.1

When you run onto something interesting, drop everything else and study it.[25] (p. 222)

Author Note:

This is an example of Skinner's humor. Embedded in it is something important. Skinner was never happy with what to him were the ponderous experimental methods of traditional psychology (See "Statistics"). Thus this quote, which comes from a 1956 autobiographical paper.

Unformalized Principle of Scientific Practice No.2

Some ways of doing research are easier than others.[25] *(p. 223)*

Author Note:

Skinner was a great builder of laboratory apparatus. Some have suggested that his facility in constructing experimental chambers for rats and pigeons (as well as teaching machines for students in elementary classrooms) was near genius.

Probably the most lasting example is the Skinner box, a training device for lower species that has been the focus of countless studies on learning. Initially the early Skinner box had to be continually operated by a person. In time Skinner devised ways to automate the apparatus including ways to vary the number of bar presses that a rat or pigeon would have to accomplish in order to get a reinforcer (a bit of food) as well as the duration of time between bar presses. These variations became known as "schedules of reinforcement."

W. Joseph Wyatt

Uniqueness of the Person

A person is not an originating agent; he is a locus, a point at which many genetic and environmental conditions come together in a joint effect. As such, he remains unquestionably unique. No one else (unless he has an identical twin) has his genetic endowment, and without exception no one else has his personal history.[5] (p. 185)

Author Note:

No psychologist has been criticized as intensely as Skinner for ignoring the "uniqueness of the person. " This is ironic because Skinner has also been equally intensely critiqued by others who feel he placed too much emphasis on the study of individual subjects in the laboratory.

The most accurate thing that can be said is that Skinner was well aware of the uniqueness of the individual. He was dedicated to studying individuals as opposed to groups of subjects. But at the same time he simply refused to agree that individuals are uniquely created by God, or are unique with respect to being in possession of, or possessed by, psychodynamic forces in the mysterious world of the mind. And he disagreed with critics whose view of human uniqueness was built on the suggestion that people are somehow not susceptible to the general laws of learning (reinforcement, punishment, extinction, etc.).

V

Value Judgements

To make a value judgment by calling something good or bad is to classify it in terms of its reinforcing effects.[3] (p. 99)

Author Note:

We make value judgements routinely and are unable to live in a world without them, Skinner believed. In contrast, humanistic psychologists such as Carl Rogers attempted to do therapy while remaining neutral regarding the client's behavior. For Skinner this was an impossible goal and, worse, an inappropriate goal in either a behavioral science or a therapeutic method.

Elsewhere Skinner asks, "With what special wisdom is the nonscientist endowed?", in response to the suggestion that behavioral scientists should not make value judgements.

Verbal Behavior (1)

Apart from an occasional relevant audience, verbal behavior requires no environmental support. One needs a bicycle to ride a bicycle but not to say "bicycle". As a result, verbal behavior can occur on almost any occasion. An important consequence is that most people find it easier to say "bicycle" silently than to "ride a bicycle silently." Another important consequence is that the speaker also becomes a listener and may richly reinforce his own behavior.[5] (p. 100)

Author Note:

One of the most intriguing aspects of our existence is language, which Skinner termed verbal behavior. He treated it in much the same way as other behavior--that is, as the result of a genetic and environmental history.

Another feature of language is that a speaker may become a listener (to his own speech). Personal observation will cause most of us to agree that this is something we do routinely.

For example, when a person says to himself, "Wow, what a nice shot. If I could only hit the golf ball like that every time," he is listening to his own verbal behavior and reinforcing his golf swing. Thus, talking to ourselves is routine, expected, and natural--and amenable to a behavioral analysis.

Verbal Behavior (2)

Universal features of language do not imply a universal innate endowment, because the contingencies of reinforcement arranged by verbal communities have universal features.[5] (p. 48)

Author Note:

Of the many theories of the origin of language, one that has received substantial attention is the linguistic theory. It holds that there are innate rules of language which cause language to emerge as it does. These innate rules are said to be in the genetic structure and to cause the emergence of language regardless of whether it is reinforced. The similarities of languages across cultures (they all have nouns, verbs, etc.) is taken by linguistic theorists as evidence for the underlying genetic structural component to language.

In this quote Skinner is arguing that the things which reinforce people are also similar across cultures and these universals are the real causes of cross-cultural sameness in language development. For example, being able to differentiate between one's self and another is reinforcing since it means that reinforcers may be directed towards oneself. Thus, it should be no surprise that all cultures have words for the first person (I, me) and other words for other persons (he, you, they).

Vernacular

Because of its similarity to the vernacular, cognitive psychology was easy to understand and the so-called cognitive revolution was for a time successful...

A version of the vernacular refined for the study of mental life is scarcely more helpful than the lay version, especially when theory began to replace introspection. Much more useful would have been behavior analysis. It would have helped in two ways, by clarifying the contingencies of reinforcement to which the vernacular alludes, and by making it possible to design better environments--personal environments that would solve existing problems and larger environments or cultures in which there would be fewer problems.[5] (p. 1210)

W. Joseph Wyatt

135

Author Note:

Skinner's abiding interest in language (verbal behavior) included his interest in what he felt was the unfortunate adoption of everyday laypersons' terms by the behavioral sciences.

This is particularly true of the school of thought known as cognitive psychology. Until his death, Skinner continued to view cognitive psychology as a dead end. This was partly because of its adoption of nonscientific terms and its elevation of those terms to the status of scientific entities that actually "exist."

Consider, for example, the use of the term memory. In the common language people frequently say things like, "I can find my way downtown and back because I have it in my memory," or a slight variation of that, "...because I remember how to do it." To Skinner such an everyday use of language by lay persons was not surprising and not to be condemned. However, it was a mistake when behavioral scientists adopted similar terms and used them as if they were scientific explanations, in Skinner's view. Cognitive scientists have done this by attempting to explain behavior with references to short-term memory, long-term memory, the storage of memories, etc.

Voluntary and Involuntary Behavior

The distinction between voluntary and involuntary behavior is a matter of the kind of control...we may say that voluntary behavior is operant and involuntary behavior reflex.[2] *(p. 112)*

Author Note:

Traditional explanations of behavior as voluntary were erroneous because they implied that the behavior was done as a result of an individual's free will. Skinner believed that all behavior is controlled and, thus, could not happen as a result of "free will." Distinctions between voluntary and involuntary behavior were illusory.

However, Skinner also held there was another way to conceptualize voluntary behavior--as operant behavior. This is the sort of behavior that a person does that results in reinforcement. While it is not done as a result of free will (a behavioral analysis could tell us the reasons--reinforcers, genetic influences, etc.), it is voluntary, at least in the sense of not being reflexive.

W

War

I recently received a letter that began "Have you ever thought about the great reservoir of feeling against war that exists throughout the world? It is being wasted! Bottled up, with nothing to show for it in terms of progress toward real peace... let us release this great reservoir of feelings." If anything can be done, it will be done not by releasing feelings but by specifying the steps to be taken to build a peaceful world. Pent-up feelings and floodgates waiting to be opened are powerful metaphors, but they do not tell us what to do.[30] *(p. 9)*

Author Note:

This discussion of war expresses both Skinner's hope that a more peaceful world can be brought about and his ideas as to how that should be done.

Because Skinner believed that feelings seldom are causes of overt behavior (rather they simply happen concurrently with observable behavior) he objected to misdirected efforts to unleash feelings in order to get things done.

He preferred a behavioral analysis of the factors that cause war, including the reinforcers for engaging in war, along with a restructured world which would make those reinforcers less likely to occur.

Welfare

Noncontingent reinforcers are characteristic of both affluence and welfare and have the same troublesome effects in both.[31] *(p. 86)*

Author Note:

To Skinner the welfare state is, to some extent, a mistake because it reinforces nonproductivity and thus works against the betterment of the culture. The same is true for affluence.

Skinner was not opposed to all forms of welfare. Rather, where possible he favored ideas such as workfare in which, if physically possible, the subsistence check was made contingent upon productive activity.

Wealth

... goods are "good" in the sense of being positively reinforcing. We sometimes speak of them also as "wealth"[2] *(p. 384)*

Author Note:

Wealth is what is reinforcing or brings reinforcers our way. This makes an important point about the nature of reinforcement and reinforcers. Skinner did not equate them with money or material possessions although these often are reinforcing.

A reinforcer is anything that increases the probability that a behavior which it follows will happen again. It may be the receipt of money or goods, but it may also be the receipt of a smile or a word of praise.

W. Joseph Wyatt

Will

As more and more of the behavior of the organism has come to be explained in terms of stimuli, the territory held by inner explanations has been reduced. The "will" has retreated up the spinal cord, through the lower and then the higher parts of the brain, and finally, escaped through the front of the head. At each stage, some part of the control of the organism has passed from a hypothetical inner entity to the external environment.[2] (p. 48-9)

Author Note:

Use of fictions such as "will" as explanations of behavior is fruitless, damaging even, in Skinner's view. This is because reference to hypothetical mental entities obscures the search for the real causes of our behavior. Skinner noted that as behavioral science explains the genetic and environmental causes of behavior, there is less to be explained by mentalistic terms such as will.

This quotation shows how individuals have attempted to locate the area of the central nervous system which houses the will, a useless and nonproductive exercise.

Witchcraft

... we may "blame" someone for an unfortunate event which was not actually the result of his behavior, although the temporal relation was such that a contingency can be asserted. "If you hadn't dawdled so, we should have started earlier, and the accident never would have happened."... We use the event as punishment... It is only a short step to

claiming the ability to arrange such contingencies. This is the underlying principle of witchcraft.[2] (p. 351)

Author Note:

When two events occur in succession we sometimes tend to attribute causal status to the first. This is not necessarily the case, though it may be on occasion. Skinner noted that the sequencing of events can at times give the perception of great power to an individual who is fairly good at manipulating time sequences.

Historically there have probably been numerous occasions on which people, cities, cultures and civilizations have been "cursed" by an individual. Occasionally some disaster soon followed, seemingly leaving the cursor with enormous power.

Writers, Artists, and Composers

Artists, composers, and writers, for example, engage in various activities which further their production... For example, crude sketches and tentative statements supply stimuli leading to other sketches and statements... Here again, it is a mistake to assume that the artist, composer, or writer is necessarily realizing some prior conception of the work he produces.[1] (p. 155)

Author Note:

To know more about the causes of great art, literature and music would mean a better world because we could then produce more of them.

Well acquainted with the arts, Skinner devoted considerable study to the ways artists achieve their inspiration.

Believing it was fruitless (and circular) to say that a creative work was produced because the artist possessed the trait of "creativity," Skinner felt that the artist could best be conceptualized as a place or location in which a unique set of genetic and environmental variables came together to produce the art. He also noted that it is evidently rather common for artists who are stuck for an idea to begin dabbling with paints, musical notes, or words on a page, which then serve as stimuli for production of more extensive artwork.

Y

Yoga

Different communities generate different kinds and amounts of self-knowledge... Existentialists, phenomenologists, and humanistic psychologists have encouraged self-observation in this search for self. Yoga has been defined as a set of practices "by which the individual prepares for liberation of the self."

... Those who seek to know themselves through an exploration of their feelings often claim an exclusive kind of knowledge... But it may be argued as well that only those who understand an experimental analysis and its use in interpreting human behavior can understand themselves in a scientific or technological sense.[5] *(p. 187-189)*

Author Note:

Skinner did not object to the use of yoga, meditation, or the like, for their relaxation value. However, he did object to looking inward in order to better know one's self. The most important knowledge about a person (that is, causes of one's behavior) lies outside the person, in the environment.

Youth of Behavior Analysis

Behavior analysis is the youngest of the three sciences (theories of natural selection and the evolution of cultures dating from the middle of the 19th century and behavior analysis only from the end of the first third of the 20th), but immaturity will not explain why it has so often been neglected. A better explanation may be that its field had been occupied for so long by that extraordinarily intriguing theory of an internal originating mind or self.[9] (p. 1209)

Author Note:

Skinner became discouraged in his later years. He earlier had hoped that behavioral sciences and ultimately the world would adopt his views more completely.

That may happen yet, but Skinner did not live to see it, having died in 1990. This quotation comes from a paper published the year of his death, in *American Psychologist* entitled "Can Psychology be a Science of Mind?" In that paper Skinner speculated on the reasons that his theoretical perspective had not been more widely adopted. He concluded that one of the major stumbling blocks was not the youth of the field but rather the strength of the long held idea that the causes of our behavior are to be found inside us, in the world of the mind, apart from the world of matter and energy with which natural sciences deal.

People tend to think of themselves in self-aggrandizing terms and desire to be "special." That view has held civilization back immeasurably, Skinner believed.

Z

Zen

A common technique of intellectual self-management is to arrange a situation - for example, a study or studio - in which there is little to interfere with a given kind of behavior... The same principle underlies the practice of Zen, in which the archer, for example, learns to minimize the particular features of a single instance. Both the artist and the archer are said to "transcend" the immediate situation; they become detached from it.[5] (p. 196)

Author Note:

That Skinner would provide a behavioral analysis of Zen is typical. He was never one to limit his analyses only to the things he observed in his laboratory. He no doubt felt that the meditation practices of Zen were important and ought to be analyzed.

Thus, to say that an individual transcends a situation through the use of meditation simply means that the individual has come under the control of the teachings of Zen, including that meditation is good and that it is powerful--so powerful that other stimuli around the individual have little or no control, at least for a time.

W. Joseph Wyatt

Zoosemiotics

Basic differences between phylogenic and ontogenic contingencies are particularly neglected in theories of communication. In the inherited signal systems of animals the behavior of a "speaker" furthers the survival of the species when it affects a "listener." The distress call of a chick evokes appropriate behavior in the hen; mating calls and displays evoke appropriate responses in the opposite sex; and so on. De Laguna has suggested that animal calls could be classified as declarations, commands, predictions, and so on, and Sebok has recently attempted a similar synthesis in modern linguistic terms, arguing for the importance of a science of zoosemiotics.[1] (p. 197)

Author Note:

Zoosemiotics, the study of language in lower species, was welcomed by Skinner. In his analysis language was defined by its effect on the listener, rather than on some presumed "meaning" of a speaker.

It is evident that Skinner approved of the study of language and language patterns in lower species. He approved of it because, as with his own studies using rats and pigeons in the laboratory, it is then possible to isolate simple learning processes. These studies would, no doubt, pave the way for understanding of more complex processes, particularly human language.

References

1. Skinner, B.F. (1969). *Contingencies of reinforcement: A theoretical analysis.* Englewood Cliffs, NJ: Prentice-Hall.

2. Skinner, B.F. (1953). *Science and human behavior.* New York: Macmillian.

3. Skinner, B.F. (1971). *Beyond freedom and dignity.* New York: Alfred A. Knopf.

4. Skinner, B.F. (1956). What is Psychotic Behavior? *Theory and treatment of the psychoses: Some newer aspects.* F. Gildea, Editor. St. Louis: Committee on Publications, Washington University, 77-99.

5. Skinner, B.F. (1974). *About behaviorism.* New York: Alfred A. Knopf.

6. Skinner, B.F. (1972). Some relations between behavior modification and basic research. *Cumulative record: A selection of papers, 3rd ed.* New York: Appleton-Century-Crofts.

7. Skinner, B.F. (1958). Reinforcement today. *American Psychologist*, 13, 94-99.

8. Skinner, B.F. (1968). Teaching science in high school-What is wrong? *Science*, 159, 704-710.

9. Skinner, B.F. (1990). Can psychology be a science of mind? *American Psychologist*, 45, 1206-1210.

10. Skinner, B.F. (1969). Contingency management in the classroom. *Education*, 90, 93-100.

11. Skinner, B.F. (1961). Why we need teaching machines. *Harvard Educational Review*, 31, 377-398.

12. Skinner, B.F. (1957). The experimental analysis of behavior *American Scientist*, 45, 343-371.

13. Skinner, B.F. (1972). Compassion and ethics in the care of the retardate. *Cumulative record: A selection of papers, 3rd ed.*, New York: Appleton- Century-Crofts.

14. Skinner, B.F. (1956). A debate with Carl Rogers. *Science*, 124, 1057-1066.

15. Skinner, B.F. (Winter, 1955-56). Freedom and the control of men. *American Scholar*, 25, 47-65.

16. Skinner, B.F. (1963). Operant behavior. *American Psychologist*. 18, 503-515.

17. Skinner, B.F. Psychology in the year 2000. Detroit: Wayne State University Press.

18. Skinner, B.F. (April 1969). The machine that is man. *Psychology Today*, 20-25, 60-63.

19. Skinner, B.F. (1966). Contingencies of reinforcement in the design of a culture. *Behavioral Science*. 11, 159-166.

20. Skinner, B.F. (1966). An operant analysis of problem solving. *Problem solving: Research, method and theory*, B. Kleinmuntz, editor, New York: John Wiley & Sons, Inc, 225-257.

21. Skinner, B.F. (1966). Some responses to the stimulus "Pavlov". *Conditional Reflex*, 1, 74-78.

22. Skinner, B.F. (1945). The operational analysis of psychological terms. *Psychological Review*, 52, 270-277.

23. Skinner, B.F. (1968). Creative student. *The technology of teaching*. Inglewood Cliffs, N.J.: Prentice-Hall.

24. Skinner, B.F. (1980). Practical eisegesis (1980). *Notebooks*. Inglewood Cliffs, N.J.: Prentice-Hall.

25. Skinner, B.F. (1956). A case history in scientific method. *American Psychologist*, 11, 221-233.

26. Skinner, B.F. (1969).   Utopia and human behavior. *Moral problems in contemporary society*, Paul Kurtz, editor. New York, Prentice-Hall, Inc.
27. Skinner, B.F. (1947).   Current trends in experimental psychology (1947).   *Current trends in psychology.* Pittsburgh: University of Pittsburgh Press, 16-49.
28. Skinner, B.F. (1959).   The flight from the laboratory. *Cummulative record.* New York: Appleton-Century-Cross.
29. Skinner, B.F. (1948).   "Superstition" in the pigeon. *The Journal of Experimental Psychology*, 38, 168-172.
30. Skinner, B.F. (1973).   Are we free to have a future? *Impact*, 3, 5-12.
31. Skinner, B.F. (Sept., 1977).   Between freedom and despotism. *Psychology Today*, 80-82, 84, 86, 90-91.

Additional Reading

Nye, R.D. (1979). *What is B.F. Skinner really saying?* Englewood Cliffs, NJ: Prentice-Hall.

Skinner, B.F. (1976). *Particulars of my life.* New York: Alfred A. Knopf.

Skinner, B.F. (1979). *The shaping of a behaviorist.* New York: Alfred A. Knopf.

Skinner, B.F. (1983). *A matter of consequences.* New York: Alfred A. Knopf.

The book by Nye is a brief overview of Skinner's work and theory. The three books by Skinner comprise his autobiography.

INDEX

Acknowledgements

Much appreciation is expressed to Barbara Wyant who typed the manuscript.

I gratefully acknowledge the following publishers for allowing use of the quotations by B.F. Skinner:

1. Sources 1, 6, 13, 15, 23, 24 and 28 were reproduced with permission of the B.F. Skinner Foundation and the B.F. Skinner family, Morgantown, WV.
2. Excerpts from Source 2, *Science and Human Behavior* ©1953, renewed 1981, are reproduced with permission of Prentice Hall, Upper Saddle River New Jersey.
3. Excerpts from Source 4 are reproduced with permission of Washington University Press, St. Louis.
4. Excerpts from Sources 7, 9, 16, 22, 25 and 29 are reproduced with permission of the American Psychological Association, Washington, DC.
5. Excerpts from Sources 8 and 14 are reprinted with permission of the American Association for the Advancement of Science, Washington, DC.
6. Excerpts from Source 10 are reproduced with permission of Project Innovation, Chula Vista, CA.
7. Excerpts from Source 11 are reproduced with permission of *Harvard Educational Review*, Cambridge, MA.
8. Excerpts from Source 19 are reproduced with permission of the International Society for the Systems Sciences, San Diego, CA, and the B.F. Skinner Foundation.
9. Excerpts from Sources 18 and 31 are reproduced with

To order additional copies of *B.F. Skinner From A to Z* or to order *The Millennium Man* complete the form below and send it with your payment or purchase order to:

Third Millennium Press
P. O. Box 844
Hurricane, WV 25526

Name: _____

Address: _____

_____

_____

Book Title	Number Copies	Cost Per Unit	Total
B.F. Skinner From A to Z :			
Softbound (0-9663622-0-9)	_____	@$10.00	_____
Hardbound (0-9663622-4-1)	_____	@$24.00	_____
Hardbound (Libraries & Institutions)	_____	@$30.00	_____
The Millennium Man			
Softbound (0-96636622-2-5)	_____	@$10.00	_____
Hardbound (0-9663622-5X)	_____	@$24.00	_____
Hardbound (Libraries & Institutions)	_____	@$30.00	_____

Sub Total _____
Plus $2.00 Per Book S&H _____
Total Enclosed _____